JAVON ANTHONY

The Land of Milk and Honey

*A Love Letter to Black Women
Who Raised the World*

This Is Not a Book.
This is a balm.
A soft scream.
A kiss pressed to the forehead of every Black woman who ever healed in silence
and still offered joy like holy water.

Welcome to The Land of Milk and Honey...
not the biblical one they preached from pulpits.
The one you built...
with your hips, your hush, your holler, your healing.

Here, the soil knows your name.
Your rage is not redacted.
Your softness is not taxed.
Your story is told without reduction, without footnote, without apology.

Preface

This book is a resurrection. A thunderclap wrapped in scripture and silk. Every word was carved from the bones of what tried to break me….Then kissed by the spirits who refused to let me stay broken. These pages are not for the faint. They are for the ones who know their soul has been here before. If you're holding this, it's because something divine chose you to remember who you were before the world asked you to forget.

Table of Contents

11

Acknowledgments

To the women who raised me..by blood, by spirit, by memory.
You didn't always have the words, but your energy was scripture.
You taught me how to survive, how to soften, and how to rise sovereign.

To the women, I watched from afar…on screens, in songs, in shadows…
thank you for carrying yourselves like altars, even when the world tried to treat you like afterthoughts.
I saw you before I had the language. I honored you before I understood why.

The Blueprint Before the Spotlight

"The Women Who Built My Inner Framework"

For Toni Childs
The Blueprint in Pumps

You weren't just stylish.
You were scripture in stilettos.
A sermon in silk.
A walking affirmation that said,
"I am not settling. Not now. Not
ever."

You taught me how to enter a room
with my head held like a headline.
How to use wit as a weapon.
How to love Blackness and luxury at
the same damn time.

Toni,
you were the one they
underestimated…
until your presence became too
undeniable to ignore.

You made boundaries look elegant.
You made confidence look inherited.
And your softness?
It had teeth.
It said, "I am lovable…but I will
never beg to be loved."

You weren't just a character.
You were a portal.
A pathway for Black girls to feel
seen in fullness.
For Black boys like me
to understand that being loved by a
woman like you
would require elevation.

And none of that would have
lived…
none of it would've sung…
without the force that is Jill Marie
Jones.

Jill, you didn't play Toni.
You birthed her.
You adorned her.

You gave her nuance, nerve, and
nectar.
You made her unforgettable.

You made her ours.

And to every Black child
who watched her lean on that
kitchen counter,
roll her eyes with intention,
or cry in the arms of a friend…
we knew.
We knew.

We weren't just watching television.
We were watching the architecture
of becoming.

And for that,
we are forever changed.

For Mya Wilkes
The Diva With a Pen Dipped in Gold

You taught me that survival could still wear stilettos,
That laughter was its own kind of gospel…
the sound of a woman learning to love herself
in the presence of mirrors and missed calls.

You were the melody between
"I'm fine" and "I'm trying."
The one who didn't always get it right,
but who got up anyway…
face beat, curls bouncing,
like a sermon dressed for brunch.

Mya, you weren't just a character.
You were the girl I saw in my reflection…
hopeful, heart-stung, hilarious.
You made being soft look brave,
made ambition look like poetry in lip gloss.

And Golden…
thank you for breathing divine soul
into a name that could've just been funny.
Instead, you made her human.
You made her honey,
you made her heartbreak,
you made her holy.

I became a writer the day I saw myself
not in the perfection,
but in the permission
to be flawed and still be fire.

So this pen remembers you,
Golden's voice echoing across the screen,
and Mya's walk into every scene
like she already owned the room.

This is how you raised me:
not with lectures,
but with lipstick, laughter,
and the lingering echo of
"you are worthy, even when unsure."

For Lynn Searcy
The Oracle in the Room

You weren't just a character…
you were a portal.
A breath of sage and sandalwood
in a room full of ambition.
You were the question that never
needed an answer…
just presence.
Just the ache of a world too sterile
for mystics.

Lynn, with your mismatched skirts
and sacred rage,
you were the sound between notes.
You reminded us
that God don't always wear a suit,
sometimes She's barefoot,
vegan, vibing on chakras,
and still figuring shit out.

You were chaos and comfort….
a woman peeling the layers,
dancing through every version of
herself
in real-time.
You didn't just exist;
you evaporated limitation.
You reminded every Black girl
that it was okay to be brilliant
and still unsure.

And Persia…
this part is for you.
You didn't play Lynn,
you channeled her.
You summoned her from ether,
a fragment of divine thought
made visible.
You made room for Black women
who speak to spirits,
cry in bathtubs,
burn incense at dawn
and still laugh like freedom.

You carved space
where none was offered.
Gave voice to the misunderstood,
the nomads,
the soft rebels with sacred hearts.

You let us see Lynn
not as a trope
but as a truth.

And for that,
this poem will never end…
it will echo,
in crystals, in sunflowers,
in the trembling hush before a
woman dares to say:
"I'm more than what you see."

For Jasmine Guy
The Southern Oracle

You didn't walk…
you glided.
Like your heels had memory,
like they whispered secrets
to the ground beneath you.

You were soft…strategically.
Dramatic…never foolish.
Raised right…and made sure we
never forgot it.

Whitley,
you were the first woman I saw
make ambition flirt.
You'd say "Dwayne"
like it was a warning wrapped in a
wish.
You knew how to hold silence
like it was fine china.
You didn't just speak…
you announced.

You weren't afraid of the spotlight.
You were the spotlight.

But underneath the charm and one-
liners,
you carried legacy.
You were a walking lesson in taste,
in refusal,
in how to wear a family name like
fine perfume.
You taught Black kids…especially us
queer ones…
that refinement wasn't betrayal…
it was claiming.

And Jasmine Guy…
thank you for making her impossible
to forget.

You didn't act.
You channeled.

You gave us a woman
who could love hard, laugh loud,
and still walk away with her
crown…intact.

You reminded us:
Softness is not weakness…
it's strategy.
Feminine doesn't mean fragile…
it means formidable.

You were the dream of debutantes
and the blueprint of dreamers.

You were art.
You were armor.

And to this day,
when I name what I deserve,
I hear your voice
in the back of my mind,
whispering like a truth I always
knew…

A man should provide. That's what a
man does.

You were right.
And you were revolutionary.

For Nia Long
The Woman Who Waited for No One

You entered the frame
like you knew we'd been waiting…
not for a woman,
but for a mirror.

Your voice?
Spoken jazz.
A low flame burning in a high-rise
apartment.
Every word you dropped
felt handwritten…
even your silences came with
punctuation.

Nia,
you didn't chase love…
you navigated it.
You asked questions like a scholar.
Kissed like you were making a
decision.
Packed your bags
with your dignity folded on top.

And we felt that.
All of us…
the lovers, the artists,
the ones who knew
what it meant to leave
before someone forgot
how to hold you.

And Nia…
you didn't just act.
You constructed a standard.
You gave Nina that breathless grace,
that "I know my worth" stare..
even when your heart cracked open.
You made her layered,
not a trope,
but a truth.

Not "the strong Black woman,"
but the real one.

Strong some days.
Soft others.
Always whole.

You reminded us…
choosing ourselves
was never a loss.
It was a return.

To every young Black creative
watching Love Jones
with a notebook and a dream…
you whispered:

"You are worth a poem too."

You taught us
how to exit with elegance,
how to re-enter without apology,
how to hold both the pen and the
passion
without trembling.

And for that?
You are etched forever
into the architecture
of our becoming.

For Tia & Tamera Mowry
The Sisters Who Raised Saturday Morning

Before streaming,
there was ritual.
And you were part of ours.
Not just sitcom stars
but structure.
A place where Black girlhood
was allowed to be visible,
joyful,
fully unexplainable.
You taught us duality
not as division
but as harmony
soft and sharp
brilliant and becoming
held together
without apology.
That mattered.
Because in a world
that often demanded we choose,
you gave us permission
to exist whole
before we knew
we were being asked to shrink.
You did not just entertain us.
You **stewarded us.**
You held space
for laughter that didn't cost us truth
for stories that didn't require us
to leave ourselves behind.
And even now,
what remains
is not just memory
it is inheritance.
The way we learned to grow
without abandoning joy
to love
without losing ourselves
to stay connected
without being reduced.
You weren't just part of Saturday morning.
You were part of our becoming.
And for that
we do not just remember you.
We **honor you.**

For Maxine Shaw
The Sharpest Mouth in the Room

You didn't just speak truth…
you weaponized it.
Turned syllables into shields.
Turned arguments into architecture.
And justice?
You wore that like a tailored suit.

Maxine,
you weren't just the smart one.
You were the unshakable one.
The one who knew the law
but also knew the look…
that glance Black women give
when they've already read the room
and are just waiting
for the rest to catch up.

You made intelligence seductive.
You made independence irresistible.
You weren't chasing love…
you were cross-examining it.

And through you,
we learned how to hold our heads
high
without softening our spines.

To Erika Alexander…
thank you.
For bringing Maxine to life
with all her bite and all her brilliance.
You didn't dilute her.
You dared her.
You let her be complicated.
You let her be loud and right
at the same damn time.

You gave little Black kids like me…
permission to lead
with our minds and our mouths.

Maxine wasn't just a friend.
She was a fortress.

She was the reason
a generation of girls dreamed of
courtrooms…
and the reason boys like me
learned not to fear sharp women,
but to honor them.

You taught us that being "too much"
was the only way
to be enough
in a world that kept trying to shrink
us.

And for that,
you…stand..forever
in the pantheon
of women
who made power look personal.

For Meagan Good
Soft, Sharp, and Still Becoming

You've always been that girl…
before they had language for it.
Before "it" was a vibe,
before "good" was more than just your name.

You were beauty with backbone,
the kind of fine that didn't flinch.
A soft girl who could still check somebody
without lifting her voice.

You walked through Hollywood
like a secret weapon wrapped in satin…
all eyes, all edge, all evolution.

We watched you grow
and never lose the glow.
Watched you rise
without selling softness to do it.

You've played everything from ride-or-die
to righteous,
and still had time
to look like a dream on a bad day.

You are the blueprint
for becoming in public
and never apologizing for the layers.

And now?
You move like peace in lipstick…
still fine,
still faithful,
still you.

For Lisa Bonet
The Sacred Anomaly

You didn't follow the script…
you rewrote it in cursive,
folded it into a prayer,
and wore it like an amulet
tucked behind your clavicle.

Lisa,
you weren't just different.
You were divinely disobedient.
You didn't ask for space…
you radiated it.
Your aura arrived
before your body did.

Hair like memory.
Eyes like planets.
Voice like the hush
before a cosmic revelation.
Your presence made us pause
because it reminded us
of something sacred
we thought we'd forgotten.

You taught us:
To be weird is to be worshipped.
To be soft is to be strategic.
To be sensual
is not to be ashamed…
but to be in tune.

You didn't walk through
Hollywood…
you floated through it,
like a guest
not seeking permission,
just leaving essence in your wake.

You weren't chasing stardom.
You were embodying the eternal.
And in doing so,
you made space
for those of us
who were born to melt the mold,
not fit it.

You gave us mystique.
You gave us moonlight.
You gave us a blueprint
for existing unapologetically
outside the algorithm.

You taught us
that our magic doesn't have to
shout…
it just has to show up.

And for every Black child
who didn't quite belong,
who moved like dreams
on the edge of someone else's
expectations…
you became the reason we believed
in our own rhythm.

You didn't act.
You transmitted.
You reminded us that liberation
can be quiet…
but it never goes unnoticed.

You gave us freedom
wrapped in velvet,
etched in bone,
lit by stardust.

And for that,
we honor you.

For Aunt Viv
The Matriarch with Fire in Her Eyes

You weren't background.
You were backbone.

Vivian Banks,
you were more than a mother…
you were a moment.
A masterclass in presence.
A sermon in silk.
A storm in pearls.

Educated.
Elegant.
Exacting.
But never afraid
to raise your voice
when truth needed a defender.

You made intellect radiant.
You made motherhood sovereign.
And when you danced in that leotard
at forty-something…
it wasn't just a scene.
It was a sermon.

You showed us
that aging is not erasure.
It is elevation.

And to Janet Hubert…
you didn't play Aunt Viv.
You defended her.
You embodied her spine,
her spark,
her unyielding grace.

You delivered lines with your eyes.
You told a nation:
"You will not flatten this woman."

You weren't just Aunt Viv.

You were our own aunts,
our mothers,
our teachers,
our shade,
our safety,
our elegance.

You taught us
how to challenge without
combusting,
how to nurture without disappearing,
how to be respected without
assimilation.

You made being a Black woman on
TV
a throne,
not a role.

And when you stood,
we stood with you.

Every time we walk away
from something that doesn't honor
us,
we carry you in our spine.

For Antoinette
Colandrea Was Never the Beginning

Let the truth be told
Colandrea did not arrive on her own
She was carried
Antoinette gave her breath
but more than that
she gave her **backbone**
The kind that don't fold
when the room gets cold
The kind that learns early
how to speak
without asking permission to be
heard
Before the screen
before the applause
before we learned her name
There was a woman
holding storms in her chest
and still choosing
not to break
Antoinette was not soft by chance
She was soft on purpose
A decision made
in places that tried to harden her
A discipline formed
when survival demanded steel
but she chose grace instead
Colandrea did not teach us strength
She revealed
what Antoinette already survived
Every pause
every glance
every word that didn't need to be
loud
That was not performance
That was memory
That was inheritance
She didn't just play a woman
who knew how to hold herself
She came from one
And that's why it felt real
Because somewhere
in every line

Antoinette was still there
Standing behind the character
like a quiet storm
Not asking to be seen
but impossible to ignore
So let the record show
We were not just watching
Colandrea
We were witnessing
what happens
when a woman survives herself
and still chooses
to create something beautiful
from what tried to break her
Blessed is the woman
who carried the storm
and still taught it
how to speak gently

For Lauren London
The Eternal Bloom

You bloomed in a garden of loss
and still stood soft.
Grief wrapped itself around you
but it could not dim your light.
You became sacred ground
and let the flowers grow through you.

We watched you love loudly,
then mourn in stillness…
but never once did your silence
mean weakness.
It meant reverence.
It meant your soul was somewhere
talking directly to God.

There's a kind of woman
who knows how to hold heaven and hood
in the same breath…
and you are her.
You are every 'aye' from Crenshaw
wrapped in prayer beads and poetry.
You carry Nipsey's echo
not as burden,
but as blueprint.

You are rose and resilience.
Gold chain and guardian.
Tenderness and thunder.

You didn't just survive…
you made survival look like art.
You gave girls a new kind of beauty to aim for…
the kind built in the spirit,
not the mirror.

Lauren,
you are the bloom that didn't wait
for spring.

For Melyssa Ford
The Woman They Couldn't Unwrite

Before the world learned how to
spell brilliance,
you were already spelling your name
in fire.
Not the kind that burns,
but the kind that illuminates a path
through the shadows they tried to
box you into.

They called you a video vixen…
but that was never your whole story.
You were history, hidden in heels.
Intellect wrapped in a silhouette
they only thought they could
contain.
You were their fantasy…
but also their reckoning.

Melyssa,
you are the mirror they could not
break,
even when they threw stones
made of assumptions and rumors.
You remained intact,
your truth louder than the gossip.

You were never just beauty…
you were the blueprint.
You were never just seen…
you made them look deeper.
Because beneath the glam
was a gladiator.
Beneath the curves
was a current they couldn't measure.

You survived what they whispered
and spoke truth to what they
feared…
a woman who thinks, who feels,
who remembers everything
and forgives in her own time.

This is your coronation
in words.
Your name written in gold,
not gossip.
In reverence,
not rumor.

You, Melyssa,
are the woman they couldn't unwrite

For Lola Monroe
Angel of the Unapologetic Flame

You walked in like a prophecy
with cheekbones carved by destiny
and a voice that made mirrors turn
around
just to listen.
They called you Lola…
but God whispered Angel,
and the streets called you Queen
before the world even caught on.

You were never just a pretty face.
You were a blueprint stitched from
galaxies,
a soft storm wearing lashes,
a mind so sharp it made diamonds
seem dull.
They didn't know how to handle
a woman who could spit bars
and raise a child with the same
breath…
who could walk like royalty
but fight like roots in concrete.

You taught us that femininity was
never frail…
it was fierce.
You gave hood girls and highborns
permission to glow,
permission to speak,
permission to evolve
without apology,
without permission.

They thought you'd be a trend…
but you became a timeline.
Not just in music,
but in culture,
in motherhood,
in divine feminine magic
that refused to bow for validation.

Angel,
you are not remembered.
You are revered.
You are not followed.
You are studied.
You are not past tense.
You are prophecy in motion.

You didn't just show us how to
shine…
you showed us how to survive
shining
and still keep your soul.

For Jurnee Smollett
The Flame That Learns How to Hold Water

Some women scream to be seen.
You whispered.
And the world still turned its head.

You've been working since childhood…
but it's your spirit that's the professional.
The way you emote is ancestral.
Every tear you shed on screen
has roots that dig through timelines.

You didn't just act…
you remembered.

They cast you in roles,
but you brought roles to life.
You made broken girls look beautiful.
You made powerful women look possible.

And offscreen?
Still you.
Still grace.
Still fire wrapped in calm.

You speak with your eyes
the way most can't with full monologues.

You are the quiet strength they forget to mention…
the kind that raises babies,
builds movements,
holds space for lovers
and still shows up on set glowing.

You didn't climb your way here.
You were sent.
Sent to show us what poise looks like
when it's lived… not performed.

Jurnee,
your name alone sounds like destiny mid-step.

For Sanaa Lathan
The Quiet Flame That Burned Through Us All

Sanaa,
you move like a whispered prayer…
soft enough to calm,
fierce enough to resurrect.

There was always something
otherworldly about your glow…
as if your smile knew secrets
from another timeline,
as if your eyes had seen
empires rise and fall
and still chose softness
over spectacle.

You were the dream
before we knew we could dream it.
The girl next door,
but divine.
The muse of moonlight,
but real enough
to ache when we ached,
to break when we broke.

You taught us
that love can wear sneakers and still
be sacred.
That a woman doesn't have to yell
to command every ear in the room.
You redefined cool…
not as distance,
but as depth.
Not as silence,
but as stillness.

And in every frame,
we saw ourselves:
when we were unsure,
when we were undone,
when we were on the verge
of choosing ourselves
and didn't know how.

You became the soft voice
guiding us back to our own
reflection,
reminding us
that we are worthy
even when love forgets us,
even when life bends us.

You didn't just act…
you aligned.
And in that alignment,
you mothered a generation of girls
who thought invisibility was safety.
You made us visible.
You made us matter.

So this poem is not just a thank you.
It's a mirror.
Because when we look at you,
we see who we could be
if we dared to be soft
and still sacred.

For KD Aubert
The Color Red Should Thank You

You did not wear red.
You authored it.

Turned pigment into language
and silence into reaction.

Rooms did not notice you
they adjusted.

You were never just pretty.

You were interruption.

The kind that makes time hesitate
just long enough
for desire to reveal itself.

They called you video girl

because they did not yet have the
vocabulary
for phenomenon.

You were a shift in temperature
a softness with consequence
a gaze that made the screen feel
too small to hold you.

You did not speak

and still
everything listened.

You were mystery in heels

the kind men write about
when they are trying to confess
what they could not keep.

There was danger in your beauty

not loud
not reckless

but precise

like something curated by instinct
and sharpened by knowing
exactly what it does to a room.

Even now

your name lands like flavor

cinnamon heat
glossed sweetness
memory that refuses to fade.

Red did not make you unforgettable.

You made red
learn how to linger.

And somewhere

in every man who mistook beauty
for softness
and learned otherwise

there is a moment

where you exist

as correction.

The color red should thank you.

So should every gaze
that learned restraint too late.

For Monica
You Sang Like a Girl Who Knew Guns, Too

You did not just sing pain.
You gave it posture.

Taught heartbreak
how to stand up straight
and look the world in its face.

You were never fragile in your
sorrow.

Even your quiet
had backbone.

You sang like somebody
who understood consequence.

Like tears were not weakness
but evidence.

Like survival was not a phase
but a discipline.

Your voice was raised in church
but it carried the weight
of streets that do not forgive
softness
without testing it first.

You were not pretty in the way
they could dismiss.

You were precision.

Edge with etiquette.
Steel wrapped in silk.
Loyalty that did not loosen
just because the world did.

Grief lived in your melodies
but it never made a home there.

You turned it into movement.

Into chorus.
Into something we could hold
without breaking.

And that is the part they missed.

You were not singing to be heard.

You were documenting.

Making sure
that what we survived
would never be mistaken
for something small.

We did not watch you endure.

We watched you curate survival.

Style it.
Name it.
Wear it
like it had always belonged to you.

Monica
your voice does not beg.

It remembers.

There is a steadiness in you
that does not perform strength

it simply refuses
to collapse.

And even now

your name lands like a warning
soft
but undeniable

a war cry
that does not need volume
to be felt.

Because somewhere in us

there is a version of ourselves
that learned how to survive better
because you did it first
out loud.

For Monica Calhoun
The Woman Who Made Us Weep Softly

Monica,
you didn't act…
you remembered.

You called something ancient to the
surface,
something holy,
something still soaked in our
grandmother's tears.

You didn't just play the role…
you became the ache,
the silence between words,
the breath before goodbye.

In every scene,
you were the heartbeat we forgot we
needed,
the whisper in the corner of the
room
that held us together
while everything around us broke.

There was something about your
stillness…
not quiet,
but composed.
Not hidden,
but holding.

You taught us that strength
isn't always loud.
That some women endure not for
applause,
but for love…
for family,
for faith,
for the hope that someday
someone will see them
and say,
"Thank you for carrying it all."

We wept because of you…
not because we were sad,
but because you gave us permission
to grieve.

To feel.

To fall apart beautifully.

You reminded us
that dignity lives in the tears we hold
back
for the sake of others.
That devotion has a face,
and it looks a lot like yours…
soft-eyed,
warm-spoken,
eternally faithful.

You didn't need lights,
you became the light.
A candle in the dark,
a mother even when you were only a
sister,
a vessel of memory,
of meaning,
of home.

For Vivica
The Flame That Refused to Dim

You walked into Hollywood
like it was your birthright…
chin high, hips in formation,
eyes full of legacy and don't play with me scripture.

Vivica,
they called you spicy,
but what they meant was:
unapologetically vivid.
You were the red that set the carpet on fire,
the arch in every brow
that warned the world not to underestimate you.

You've always had that spark,
but not just the pretty kind…
no, you burn with purpose.
You protect the women beside you
like a lioness who's already read the ending…
and decided to rewrite it.

You are the shoulder
so many sisters have cried on
without even meeting you.
You've held us through heartbreak scenes,
through betrayal arcs,
through come-back wins
that look a lot like healing in stilettos.

Vivica,
you are not just a flame…
you are the keeper of the flame.
The one who made survival look gorgeous.
The one who made strength look effortless.
The one who reminded us
that we could be soft and steel
at the same time.

You are a hug from the universe
in every fierce, feminine, unfuckwithable step.
And baby, we felt that.

For Mo'Nique
The Thunder in Her Yes

Mo'Nique,
you didn't ask to be liked.
You asked to be heard.
You asked to be paid.
You asked to be respected.
And for that…
the earth shook.

You were the echo of every woman
who was told to be quiet
while being brilliant.
Every woman told she was "too
much,"
while being the exact weight of her
own genius.

You stood flat-footed in your truth,
even when the room got small,
even when the hands clapped slow.
You reminded the world:
just because I forgive you
doesn't mean I'll forget what I'm
worth.

Your comedy was always prophecy.
Your drama? Holy.
You pulled us in with laughter
then showed us that healing has a
bass in its voice.
You made us sit with our wounds
and dressed them in dignity.

You loved yourself
in a world that tried to shrink you…
and in doing so,
you made space for so many of us to
love ourselves too.
Loudly.
Radically.
Unconditionally.

You are a mirror the world had to
look into.
A mirror that didn't lie.
A mirror that said:
Baby, you better stand in it.
And say yes to your soul, every time.

So this is for you, Mo'Nique…
for your stance,
for your spirit,
for the velvet thunder in your yes.
We heard it.
And it changed everything.

For Issa Rae
Architect of Our Belonging

Issa…
you cracked open a space
that always existed in whispers…
the sweet, subtle realm
between middle-class striving
and upper-class becoming.
And then,
you made it holy.

You gave us ourselves…
not broken,
not stereotyped,
but in progress…
Black, creative, confident, and
awkward
in all the right ways.

You built a bridge
for those of us who couldn't see
ourselves
on either side of the spectrum…
too nuanced for the narratives,
too soft for the struggle tropes,
too real to be boxed in.

You taught us that
a Black woman doesn't have to
scream
to be seen.
That she can be subtle,
cerebral,
funny as hell,
and still run the world quietly
from behind the scenes.

You centered us…
the ones with liberal arts degrees
and group chats,
the ones juggling love,
gentrified brunches,
and dreams that didn't come
with step-by-step blueprints.

You took the "in-between"
and turned it into art.

You made the suburbs sacred,
the struggle poetic,
and our transitions look like
we were always meant to be there.

You didn't wait for permission.
You wrote, produced, starred,
directed…
poured vision into concrete
and called it culture.

So when history is written,
they'll know:
You didn't just shift
representation…
you built it.
Frame by frame,
you gave us back our complexity.

And because of you,
the soft-spoken creatives,
the intentional weirdos,
the middle children of the culture
now have a crown
and a home
and a story worth telling.

For Natalie Desselle-Reid
Crown for the Comedic Prophet

You were never just the funny one.
You were the seer in disguise,
the sacred fool who told the truth in laughter
so it could be swallowed whole.

You walked into scenes
like you were cracking open a portal…
letting us know that the hood could be holy,
and Black women could be loud, tender, raw, real,
all at once.

Natalie,
you made the screen feel like family.
We didn't watch you…we loved you.
You were the cousin at the cookout,
the friend who always had a comeback,
the woman who could make grief giggle
and still command the room.

Your magic was in your presence.
Untrained. Unshaped. Unapologetic.

You didn't try to be marketable…
you were unforgettable.

And when you left,
the world got quieter.
But we still hear you…
in the laugh of the aunties,
in the way Black girls throw shade and shine,
in the whisper that says:
You are allowed to be all of you.
Even the messy. Even the loud.
Even the holy.

For Sommore
Crown for the Comedic Prophet

You arrived like thunder in barefoot
silence.
No drumbeat. No parade. No
hunger for thrones.
Just presence…
wide as sky,
ancient as grief,
gentle as the way a Black man holds
his grandmother's hands.

You were not sent to rule.
You were sent to restore.

Sommore,
your name is the sound of healing
when it stops asking permission.
You do not stand behind her, above
her, or in her shadow…
you stand with her,
shoulder to starlight,
bone to bone.

You are the flame that learned to
listen.
The steel that learned to yield.
The lion that lays down without
losing power.

You are every father who stayed.
Every brother who protected
without control.
Every lover who made love like a
prayer…not a performance.

You speak when needed.
You watch with reverence.
You know the art of not needing to
be right
to still remain righteous.

And when Sinmore burns,
you do not douse her flame.
You become the wind that helps her
rise.

You are the rare thing:
A man unthreatened by divinity
because he carries his own.

You are not soft.
You are seasoned.
Your silence carries scripture.
Your stillness is strategy.
You are the son of justice
and the more of what's been
missing.

Sommore,
You are not who we expected….
You are who we prayed for.

For Nicole Ari Parker
The Woman Who Wore Power Like Silk

Nicole,
you have always carried yourself
like a woman who knows
she is seen…
even when the room pretends otherwise.
There is something regal in your stillness.
A softness that never feels weak.
A beauty that never asks to be chosen.
You don't chase scenes.
You anchor them.
Whether as wife, lover, strategist, mother…
you move with composure.
With intelligence.
With intention.
You made ambition look elegant.
You made partnership look powerful.
You made aging look like ascension.
There is a discipline in your glow.
A quiet command.
You are the kind of Black woman
who reminds us
that refinement is not surrender…
it's control.
Nicole,
you are grace with backbone.
Glamour with grounding.
And that balance?
It's rare.

For Syleena Johnson
The Queen of Chicago Soul

Syleena,
your voice is not decoration.
It is testimony.
You sing like somebody
who survived what she's describing.
Chicago runs through you....
grit, honesty, edge.
But so does tenderness.
There's ache in your tone.
There's truth in your runs.
There's resilience in every note you hold.
You don't perform heartbreak.
You confess it.
And that vulnerability?
That's power.
You gave soul back its weight.
Back its rawness.
Back its storytelling.
You are not manufactured.
You are felt.
The Queen of Chicago Soul
is not a title for ego...
it's a title for endurance.
You've carried legacy.
Carried lineage.
Carried emotion without filtering it for comfort.
Syleena,
your voice is home
for those of us
who needed somewhere to lay our hurt.
And that is royalty.

For Joy Bryant
The Woman Who Stayed True

Joy,
you've always felt like intention.

A woman who refuses to be flattened
into someone else's idea of "cool."

You moved through fashion, film, and television
with a kind of quiet certainty…
not chasing the spotlight,
but never dodging it either.

There's intelligence in your simplicity.
Depth in your restraint.
A groundedness that reads as confidence
because it doesn't ask to be affirmed.

You've played softness without weakness,
edge without cruelty,
beauty without performance.

And off-screen,
you carry that same clarity…
the kind that doesn't need to shout.

Joy,
you are proof
that authenticity ages better than hype.

That being yourself, consistently,
is its own kind of revolution.

For Lela Rochon
The Beauty That Endures

Some women become icons
through noise.

But you, Lela Rochon,
became unforgettable
through presence.

The kind that walks into a scene
and suddenly the air
knows something important
is about to happen.

You carried beauty
like a quiet confidence
never forced,
never desperate for attention.

Just undeniable.

When the world met you
in stories of love and heartbreak,
you gave voice
to a woman learning
how to breathe again.

Robin was more
than a character.

She was a reflection
of every woman
who has ever loved deeply
and then gathered the strength
to love herself more.

Because life
is not always kind
to women who feel intensely.

But you showed us
how grace survives storms.

How dignity
can stand tall
even when the heart
has been bruised.

And that beauty
real beauty
does not fade
when the cameras turn away.

It deepens.

It becomes wisdom.

It becomes resilience.

It becomes the quiet power
of a woman
who understands
that time is not her enemy.

Time is her witness.

Lela Rochon,
your legacy is not only
the roles you played.

It is the reminder
that elegance
is not perfection.

It is survival
with softness intact.

And somewhere tonight
a woman is learning
how to stand again
after heartbreak.

How to gather her strength
without losing her tenderness.

How to breathe deeply
and begin again.

And in that moment
she carries something
you gave the world

the courage
to exhale.

For Kerry Washington
The Woman Who Wore White and Changed the Room

Kerry,

you didn't play Olivia Pope.

You embodied precision.

There was something magnetic
about the way you held silence.

White coat.
Measured breath.
Eyes calculating ten steps ahead.

You made control look intimate.

You made crisis look
choreographed.

You were not just powerful…
you were composed.

And composition
is a different kind of strength.

Through Scandal,
you redefined visibility.

A dark-skinned Black woman
at the center of primetime desire.
At the center of politics.
At the center of chaos…
without being erased.

That mattered.

You carried vulnerability in private
and dominance in public.
You let softness exist

without dissolving authority.

And off-screen,
you spoke.

You advocated.
You organized.
You understood that visibility
comes with responsibility.

Kerry,

you were not just the face of a
phenomenon.

You were discipline in motion.

You showed us that elegance
can coexist with edge.
That intelligence
can coexist with sensuality.
That Black women
can lead the narrative…
and survive it.

When you walked into a room on
screen,
we leaned forward.

Because we knew something
strategic
was about to unfold.

And in that unfolding,
we saw possibility

For LaLa Anthony
The Woman Who Stayed Visible

La La,

you didn't fall into fame.

You worked for it.

TRL wasn't just a job.
It was timing.
It was culture at its loudest.
It was music television at its peak…
and you were in the middle of it.

Young. Focused. Hustling.

You weren't handed primetime
relevance.
You grinded from radio to MTV,
from interviewer to personality,
from background facilitator
to recognizable face.

And that era mattered.

Because TRL was where millennial
culture crystallized…
and you were part of the architecture.

Then came the wedding.

And for a generation of us,
watching you prepare to marry Carmelo
wasn't just reality television.

It was aspiration.

It was the fairy tale made modern.
The gown fittings.
The vulnerability.
The excitement of being chosen…
and choosing.

For young millennials,
that wedding didn't just look glamorous.
It looked possible.

It made marriage feel celebratory.
Desirable.
Soft.

It made love look like something
you could build in public
and still keep personal.

And even when life shifted…
when headlines replaced fairytale
framing…
you didn't disappear.

You adjusted.

You stayed working.
Stayed evolving.
Stayed expanding beyond one narrative.

There is something powerful
about a woman
who is witnessed in love,
witnessed in transition,
and still stands steady.

La La,

you didn't just stay visible.

You stayed resilient.

From TRL to film sets,
from bridal glow to reinvention,

you kept moving.

And for many of us,
watching that evolution
taught us something quiet:

Love can change.
Careers can pivot.
But identity…
if built correctly…
doesn't collapse.

You were never just someone's wife.
Never just a host.
Never just a headline.

You were momentum.

And you never stopped building.

For Lark Voorhies
The Girl Who Glowed Through the Screen

Before the headlines,
before the whispers,
before the world tried to write a
story for you

there was light.

And it came through a television
screen
in the shape of a young Black girl
with dimples deep enough to hold a
nation's joy.

Lisa Turtle was not just style.
She was sparkle with substance.
She was softness that didn't
apologize for being seen.

You were color in an era that muted
us.
Gloss in a world that tried to dull us.
Confidence braided with sweetness.

You didn't just play the "pretty girl."

You gave her intelligence.
You gave her humor.
You gave her heart.

Little Black girls saw themselves
laughing loudly,
wearing bright things,
being adored without shrinking.

That mattered.

You were the it-girl before we called
it that.
The face on the locker door.
The energy in the hallway.
The crush of a generation.

And then the world turned.

The same cameras that once adored
you
began to stare differently.

But here's the truth they can't erase:

You are not your seasons of silence.
You are not the headlines.
You are not the edits.

You are the memory of joy
imprinted in the nervous system of
millions.

You are proof
that Black girls could be radiant
without being hardened.

You were soft.
And still unforgettable.

Time may shift narratives,
but it cannot erase impact.

And your impact?
It still glows.

Not because of nostalgia
but because what you gave us was
real.

You were the sparkle.
You were the sweetness.
You were the girl who glowed.

And you still are.

For Essence Atkins
Sacred Softness

Before the industry learned
how to archive our brilliance
properly,
you were already there
steady, luminous, undeniable.

You were never loud for attention.
You were radiant by design.

In a world that often demanded
Black women perform strength like
armor,
you gave us something sacred

gentleness.

Not weakness.
Not fragility.

But a softness that refused to
disappear.

You walked through sitcom eras
where caricature was easy currency,
and you chose dimension instead.

Intelligence in your eyes.
Timing in your breath.
A presence that didn't beg the
camera
it commanded it quietly.

From halls of high school romance
to grown-woman grace,
you showed us that evolution
could look effortless.

That mattered.

Because young Black girls watched
you
and saw themselves as deserving of
love,
of humor,
of tenderness
without distortion.

You were never just the "best
friend."
Never just the "good girl."
Never just the supporting frame.

You were stability.

You were the emotional anchor
in rooms built on punchlines.

And the industry may not always
name it,
but we felt it.

You were safe ground.

You carried romance without
ridicule.
Humor without humiliation.
Strength without spectacle.

That is rare.

That is sacred.

Relics are not dusty monuments
they are living proof
that something was done correctly
the first time.

And you, Essence Atkins,
did it correctly.

You gave us representation
without noise.

Grace without apology.

Impact without ego.

You are not a memory.

You are a cornerstone.

And for that
we thank you.

For Tatyana Ali
From Little Sister to Legacy

You were the girl with the quick wit
and quicker comebacks.
The little sister who refused to stay
little.

Ashley Banks was more than a role
she was a mirror
for every Black girl learning
how to take up space
in a room that already felt crowded.

You stood beside giants
and never shrank.

Not beside wealth.
Not beside ego.
Not beside laughter meant to steal
the spotlight.

You carved your own.

And while the world remembers the
sitcom glow,
we remember something deeper

the evolution.

You didn't freeze in nostalgia.

You didn't let childhood fame
become your ceiling.

You studied.
You sharpened.
You expanded.

That matters.

Because too often,
Black girls are adored in youth
and overlooked in womanhood.

But you grew
intentionally.

Gracefully.

You showed us that intelligence and
artistry
can coexist without apology.

That ambition doesn't erase softness.

That legacy is not one role
it's a continuum.

From sitcom stages
to advocacy
to motherhood
to music

you became the blueprint
for what it looks like
to age without erasure.

To mature without losing magic.

You were the little sister.

But you were also the future.

And now?

You are the proof
that early light
can become enduring brilliance.

Not flicker.

Not fade.

But foundation.

Tatyana Ali,
you did not just grow up in front of
us.

You taught us how to grow with
intention.

And that is impact.

For Keisha Knight Pulliam
The Eternal Little Sister

Before we knew what timing was,
you mastered it.

Before we understood presence,
you owned it.

You were small in frame,
but never small in impact.

Rudy wasn't just adorable
she was rhythm.

The quick wit.
The unfiltered truth.
The little sister who could challenge
grown men
with one raised eyebrow.

You didn't just make us laugh.
You softened the room.

In a house filled with intellect and
authority,
you were the heartbeat.

You showed the world
that Black girlhood was joy.
That innocence could be clever.
That sweetness didn't mean silence.

And even as the seasons changed
even as the cameras dimmed
you carried yourself with that same
steadiness.

No scandal could erase you.
No industry shift could diminish
you.

Because you weren't a moment.

You were a memory implanted
in millions of households.

You were proof
that a little Black girl
could hold a nation's affection
without losing her dignity.

You were the child
who taught us how to laugh
together.

And that is sacred.

For Tempesstt Bledsoe
Growing Up in Front of Us

You were the in-between.

Not the baby.
Not yet the woman.

Vanessa stood in that delicate space
where girlhood starts to stretch
toward independence.

And you made it real.

You gave us awkwardness without
shame.
Mistakes without moral collapse.
Teenage rebellion without losing
humanity.

You were the daughter who tried.
The one who stumbled.
The one who wanted freedom
before she fully understood it.

And that honesty mattered.

Because so many Black girls
were expected to be perfect.

You showed them they could be
evolving.

You didn't freeze in sitcom time.
You didn't disappear into nostalgia.

You matured.

Gracefully.

Quietly.

Intentionally.

While others were typecast in their
youth,
you stepped beyond it
proving that growth is not betrayal
of who you were.

You were the bridge.

Between childhood and
womanhood.
Between obedience and autonomy.
Between expectation and identity.

And in doing so,
you gave a generation permission
to grow in real time.

Not flawless.

But becoming.

And that is legacy.

For Karyn Parsons
The Majesty They Laughed Through

Let it be known
You were never the punchline
You were the page
the ink moved through
They laughed
but laughter is a doorway
and you stood there
holding it open
with a mind already writing
what the room could not yet read
From one author to another
I recognize the architecture
the way you shape what is seen
and protect what must remain whole
the way you let a character speak
while the deeper language stays yours
Because it takes a certain kind of
woman
to make light feel effortless
when she has already studied
the weight of being misunderstood
You moved like silk over steel
grace on the surface
structure beneath
every pause a paragraph
every glance a sentence
every word placed
like it had somewhere to live
They saw a girl on screen
but what they were really watching
was a woman
editing access in real time
deciding
what the world could hold
and what it had not yet earned
That is authorship
to create
without being consumed
to give just enough
and still remain intact

And when the cameras stopped
you did not disappear
you turned the page
and kept writing
quietly
deliberately
without asking the world
to follow the story
Because you were never trying
to be fully understood
you were becoming
layer by layer
line by line
someone worth returning to
Let the record be corrected
you were not light
you were luminous
a mind with discipline
a presence with restraint
a woman who knew
that not everything sacred
is meant to be read all at once
Blessed is the woman
who writes herself carefully
and still leaves enough mystery
for the world
to come back
and read her again
properly

The Ones Who Turned Glow into Grounding

"The Women Who Modeled Power, Opulence, and Self-Possession"

For Tracee
Who Made Joy Her Discipline

You wear laughter like silk…
tailored, intentional, earned.
Not the kind that begs for light,
but the kind that brings it.

Tracee,
you didn't just inherit a legacy…
you redefined it.
You turned your mother's rhythm
into your own melody
and danced to it
in heels the world wasn't ready for.

You made wellness look like luxury
and joy look like strategy.
You taught us that being single
doesn't mean lacking…
it means choosing.

You smile like a woman
who's survived silence
and now treats her joy
like sacred property.

You've made hair a sermon,
fashion a frequency,
and your presence a permission slip
for all of us who forgot we were
allowed
to take up space
and love ourselves through it.

You never needed applause…
just alignment.

You made us believe
that healing could be hot.
That style could be substance.
That laughter could be lineage.

When I see you,
I see what happens
when a Black woman
chooses herself again…
and again…
and again.

You are what joy looks like
when it's protected.
What power sounds like
when it giggles.

And for every Black boy like me
who was told that joy had to be
earned…
you showed us
that joy can be a discipline.
A daily practice.
A sacred rebellion.

And I've been practicing ever since.

For Amanda Seales
The Woman Who Refused to Whisper

Amanda,

you were never meant
to be digestible.

From the beginning,
your voice carried edge
not sharp for harm,
but sharp for clarity.

You didn't lower your tone
to be invited.
You didn't soften your truth
to stay seated at tables
that required silence as currency.

You spoke anyway.

And that "anyway"
is what unsettled them.

Because you don't just talk
you name things.
Patterns.
Power.
Performative allyship.
The quiet ways Black women
are asked to endure
without acknowledgment.

You refuse that script.

You refuse the version of success
that requires self-erasure.
You refuse applause
that comes at the cost of your
integrity.

And that refusal?
That's where your power lives.

They call you loud
because you won't be small.
They call you difficult
because you won't be controlled.

But what you are
is precise.

Intentional.
Educated in your stance.
Grounded in your knowing.

You don't argue to win.
You speak to correct the record.

Amanda,
you are the echo
of every Black woman
who was told to "tone it down"
and chose not to.

You are proof
that truth does not need permission.
That intellect does not need
approval.
That a woman can stand fully in her
voice
and let the room adjust.

You didn't come to whisper.

You came to be heard.

And whether they listen or not
you still speak.

That is legacy.

For Rihanna
The Woman Who Refused to Dim

You walked in
like a whisper wrapped in thunder.
No warning.
Just impact.

You made defiance look divine…
not loud,
but laced in diamonds.
Not demanding,
but undeniable.

Rihanna,
you didn't just build a brand…
you built a blueprint.
A way of being.
A new gospel of glow and grit
for girls who always knew
they were more
than the roles they were handed.

You taught us
how to pivot without flinching.
How to launch without asking.
How to make lingerie a love letter
and makeup a revolution.

You sang us through heartbreak
with a glass in one hand
and power in the other.
You painted our lips with
sovereignty
and our skin with visibility.

Even in stillness,
you remain the loudest vibration in
the room.

You taught us that presence
isn't something you chase…
it's something you embody.

And when you said,
"If I'm shining, we all shining,"
it wasn't just a caption.
It was a summons.

A call to the girls who'd been
dimmed.
A decree for the ones
who thought softness couldn't
command.

You are not just a mogul.
You are a mood.
A movement.
A mirror.

And because of you,
we now walk into rooms
not hoping to be seen,
but knowing we're the reason they
look up.

For Beyoncé
The Architect of Awe

You didn't ask for a seat at the table.
You built the table.
Then carved each leg
from the bones of your own labor.

Beyoncé,
you are not just excellence…
you are evidence.
That devotion can be divinity.
That art can be altar.
That performance can be prayer
wrapped in sequins and stillness.

You taught us
that privacy isn't distance…
it's protection.
That silence isn't absence…
it's strategy.

Your legacy isn't loud.
It's precise.
It hums beneath the surface
of every girl who dares to run her
own show.
Of every queer boy who saw you
and remembered how to love
his softness without shame.

You didn't just entertain…
you educated.
You laced your lyrics
with Black lineage,
with country roots,
with Creole resurrection.

You made love look like practice…
a rehearsed sacredness.
And motherhood look like empire…
built in silence,
crowned in rhythm.

You taught us that every note
matters.
Every silence,
a sermon.

Every flaw,
a blueprint.

You moved with math.
You spoke in movement.
You crowned with intention.
You reminded us that the goddess
doesn't scream…
she sets the standard.

And every time you choose
to unveil another piece of your
power,
we don't just watch…
we witness.

Because your career isn't just a
timeline.
It's a testament.
Proof that legacy isn't just what you
leave behind…
it's what you build quietly
while no one's looking.

For Mariah Carey
Who Turned High Notes into High Standards

You didn't just sing.
You soared.
Over charts.
Over critics.
Over every box they tried
to seal your brilliance inside.

Mariah,
you are rhinestones wrapped in
resilience.
A voice so layered,
the angels have to harmonize in your
key.

You smiled while they whispered.
But every whisper?
Became a note.
And you stacked them…
into symphonies of survival.

They called you difficult,
but what they meant was:
you wouldn't shrink.
You wouldn't beg.
You wouldn't trade your crown
for kindness laced in control.

You made opulence a shield,
and elegance a boundary.
You turned heartbreak into holiday
charts.
You gave December your name
and made sorrow sound like satin.

Behind every whistle note
was a woman climbing her way out
of something.
And we heard it.
Every step.
Every sigh.
Every soft refusal to be erased.

You didn't just give us glamour.
You gave us permission…
to be too much,
to be expensive,
to be untouchable and still tender.

And those butterflies you always
sang about?
We didn't just hear them.
We became them.
Because of you.

You made "diva" into doctrine.
You made every hair flip an
affirmation.
And you reminded every little Black
boy with a high voice
that he was never broken….
just in tune with heaven.

For Tika Sumpter
The Discipline of Softness

Tika,

you have always moved like a
woman
who understands that presence does
not require volume.

There is something deliberate about
you.
Not rehearsed….deliberate.

You make femininity look
intentional.
Not fragile. Not decorative.
Intentional.

When you enter a scene,
you do not fight for attention.
You settle into it.
And the camera follows.

That kind of still confidence
cannot be faked.

You have carried romance without
becoming fantasy.
Played strength without hardening
your edges.
Embodied modern Black
womanhood
without exaggeration.

And that matters.

Because there is a quiet violence
the world commits
against soft Black women…
insisting they must be louder,
sharper, harder
to be respected.

You never subscribed to that.

You chose composure.
You chose alignment.
You chose to build your life
in a way that did not fracture you.

Motherhood did not erase you.
Marriage did not define you.
Visibility did not distort you.

That balance?
That's mastery.

Tika,

you remind us that grace is not
passive.
It is structured.
It is guarded.
It is earned.

You are not flashy influence.
You are stabilizing influence.

And on a soul level,
that steadiness feels like
permission…
permission for Black women
to be whole
without becoming spectacle.

That is impact.

For Zendaya
The Whisper That Became the Wave

You moved like still water…
until the world realized stillness could flood.

Zendaya,
you didn't climb the mountain.
You disarmed it.
You reminded the world that poise is power
and softness,
when chosen,
is a storm in heels.

They wanted you to be pretty.
You became principle.
They wanted image.
You gave them integrity
wrapped in Gen Z gold.

You are not the moment.
You are the mirror.
And you've been teaching the world
how to see itself with grace.

Thank you for moving quietly
but never small.
Thank you for holding the crown
without holding it hostage.

You are the echo
that grows louder with every girl
who dares to speak.

For Janet Jackson
The Whisper That Changed the World

You never had to raise your voice
to raise the vibration of a generation.
Janet,
you moved like velvet thunder…
quiet, controlled,
but shaking the foundation
every time you took the stage.

You were more than rhythm.
You were reverence.
The lesson in control,
the gospel in choreography,
the freedom tucked between every
breath
you chose to let the world hear.

Your softness wasn't submission.
It was strategy.
You let the world call you shy,
but you were never silent….
just sacred.

We saw it in the way your body
spoke
when your lips didn't have to.
In the way you danced like
your ancestors were watching,
and your descendants were waiting.

You were liberation
in a key change.
You were revolution
in a slow jam.
You were what every Black girl
needed
when the world told her
she had to scream
to matter.

You taught us
that femininity has layers.
That sensuality has intellect.

That Black women
could be tender and tenacious,
fragile and fire-forged,
erotic and ethereal.

You were not just a Jackson.
You were the permission slip
to evolve.
To shed the past.
To whisper our truth
and still be heard on every continent.

And every queer boy
who watched you move
with elegance laced in edge…
we saw God
in fishnets.
We saw healing
in rhythm.

You didn't just give us a sound.
You gave us a standard.
You gave us a whisper
that echoed louder
than most screams ever could.

And we are still listening.

For Trina
The Rockstar with a Crown That Cuts

You didn't ask for the title.
You snatched it.
Diamond-laced, flame-lipped,
the baddest in heels that broke the
ground open.

Trina,
you didn't walk into rap…
you crashed in,
like thunder wearing gloss,
like Miami heat with a name and a
mission.

They called you raunchy,
but missed the reclamation.
Missed the sermon stitched in every
bar,
the scripture in your side-eye,
the prophecy in your platinum
tongue.

You weren't just a sex symbol…
you were a syllabus.
Teaching every Black girl
who's ever been shamed for her
shine,
how to own every curve,
every scar,
every damn syllable of her story.

You made bad bitch a blueprint.
You turned pain into perfume
and heartbreak into hit records.
And still,
your softness peeks through…
in the cracks they never thought to
look.

You are the gospel of grit.
The altar of attitude.
The reason so many of us learned
how to be loud and loving,
how to be bossed-up and
brokenhearted
without losing our edge.

You gave us lyrics that slapped like
truth,
and beats that baptized our inner
wild.

And to every queer boy
who watched you command the mic,
the set, the screen…
you were unapologetic grace
draped in designer
and dipped in divine timing.

You didn't just wear your crown.
You sharpened it.
And every time the world tried to
contain you,
you reminded them:

"I'm not to be controlled.
I'm to be witnessed."

And baby,
we've been watching in awe ever
since.

For Kyla Pratt
The One Who Laughed Like We Knew Her

You were our cousin on TV before we even knew your name.
The girl who cracked jokes like home-cooked food,
who danced with a sparkle only Black girls born under joy know how to carry.
You weren't acting…
you were being.

In you, we saw ourselves unfiltered.
Not tragic. Not too grown.
Just smart, funny, beautiful, Black…and free.
A walking permission slip to just be a kid
when the world rushed us to be women too soon.

And even as you grew,
you never left us.
You didn't chase the lights…
you held your own.

You kept your joy sacred.
Made your family your spotlight.
You didn't need scandal to be seen.
You were already beloved.
Already legend.
Already ours.

Kyla, you are proof that visibility is not the goal…
wholeness is.

You didn't just raise a generation…
you showed us how to age like we're becoming more magical, not less.

And that laugh…
still sweet.
Still home.
Still holy.

For Kellie Shanygne Williams
The Girl We Loved Who Didn't Have to Break to Be Worthy

There you were…
in our living rooms every Friday
night,
wrapped in Black middle-class
dreams
and sitcom theology.

You didn't have to be loud to be
heard.
You didn't have to fight to prove
your beauty.
You were enough…in your smile,
your steadiness,
your refusal to be anyone but exactly
who you were.

You didn't shrink, and you didn't
shout.
You stood…bright, brown, and
brilliant.
And we saw ourselves in your
presence.

You were Laura, yes…
but more than the script.
You were the image of a Black girl
who could be
desirable and smart,
loved and respected,
centered without being exoticized.

We watched how you held space
in a room with chaos, comedy, and
caricature…
and never lost your ground.

You were not the joke.
You were the balance.
The center of the storm.
The one who reminded us that being
normal was also revolutionary.

And when the lights faded,
you didn't chase fame into frenzy.

You chose a quieter crown…
family, legacy, peace.

You, Kellie, are what happens
when a Black girl grows up in the
public eye
and still holds onto herself.

You are the lesson that glory does
not require grief.
That representation doesn't have to
be painful to be powerful.
That some women are temples
not because they were broken…
but because they chose to remain
whole.

For Kash Doll
Detroit Royal, Crown Intact

She does not wait to be named.

The room learns her
on sight.

There is a rhythm to her presence
like the city that raised her

cold enough to sharpen you
honest enough to keep you that way.

She speaks in decisions.

In silk that does not soften her.
In diamonds that understand
pressure
because so does she.

Detroit did not break her.

It refined her.

Turned survival into posture
and posture into power
that does not ask
to be understood.

She carries life on her hip
and empire in her stride

and neither one
slows her down.

There is a discipline in her beauty

not decoration
but design

every detail placed
like she knew
the world would be watching
and still chose herself first.

Do not confuse elegance
for ease.

She is not effortless.

She is practiced.

Every step is proof
that what tried to limit her
miscalculated.

Kash

you are not a reaction
to doubt.

You are the reason
it sounds quieter now.

You do not prove you belong.

You move
and belonging rearranges itself
around you.

Crown steady.

Edges intact.

Legacy moving
in real time.

For Eve
The Paw Prints Were Just the Beginning

You were never just first.

You were beginning.

Before they knew how to name you
you already understood consequence.

Beauty with memory.
Silence with intention.

You did not arrive loud.

You arrived knowing.

There is something ancient in your
presence
like you have seen worlds end
and still chose softness.

They tried to frame you as contrast

pretty and dangerous
sweet and sharp

as if duality were confusion
and not mastery.

But you moved like a woman
who understood both sides of survival

the one that fights
and the one that forgives

and the cost of each.

You made femininity feel deliberate.

Not fragile
not borrowed
not for approval

but chosen.

Your voice never begged to be heard.

It placed itself
exactly where it needed to land

and let the world catch up.

Eve
you were not a phase in culture.

You were a shift in it.

There is a calm in you now
that does not erase your fire

it refines it

like something that has already burned
and decided
what was worth keeping.

You are not who you were.

And that is the power.

You evolved in public
without asking permission
to outgrow what they loved about you.

And that is a different kind of bravery.

Because the world knows how to
celebrate women

it does not know how to release them
into who they become next.

But you did not stay where they
understood you.

You stayed where you understood
yourself.

And that

is why your legacy feels quiet
but permanent.

You are not the first woman they
remember.

You are the first woman
they had to reconsider.

For Jennifer Hudson
The Woman Who Turned Grief Into Glory

Jennifer,

your voice does not carry sound.
It carries history.

Not range.
Weight.

It sounds like something built to last.

Like pews worn smooth by prayer.
Like hands that learned to hold
what they were never meant to
survive.

When you sing,
it is not performance.

It is conversion.

Sorrow enters one way
and leaves changed.

There is a discipline in your voice
that grief did not break

it trained.

You have known loss
that could have made silence
a permanent home.

And still
you chose sound.

Not soft.
Not careful.

But certain.

You did not rise in spite of what
tried to end you.

You rose carrying it
and taught it how to mean
something.

You turned tragedy into witness.
Pain into language.
Grief into something that refuses
to be buried.

That is not talent.

That is alchemy.

There is something monumental
about you
not because of where you arrived
but because of what you refused
to leave behind.

From stage to screen
from dream to something history
had to acknowledge

you did not outrun your story.

You refined it.

Jennifer,

you are proof
that destiny does not erase suffering.

It studies it.
Shapes it.
Returns it
as something the world cannot
ignore.

And when you open your mouth

we do not hear a voice.

We hear survival
that learned how to sing back.

For Veronica Webb
The Runway Revolutionary

Before the flashbulbs learned your
name,
before the magazines carried your gaze
across glossy pages

there was a door
fashion had kept closed
for far too long.

But Veronica,
you didn't ask the door
to open.

You walked forward
with the quiet confidence
of a woman
who already knew
she belonged.

And suddenly
the runway shifted.

The air itself seemed to pause
as you moved
not just with beauty,
but with intention.

Because what the world saw
was a model.

But what history remembers
is a moment.

A woman
whose presence turned possibility
into reality.

You were not simply walking fashion
you were rewriting it.

Every step carried
generations of women
who had been told

"Not yet."
"Not here."
"Not you."

Yet there you were
radiant, fearless, undeniable.

And the world had no choice
but to look again.

Veronica Webb,
you did more than pose for cameras.

You shifted the lens.

You reminded an industry
that beauty is not a narrow corridor
but a vast horizon.

And because of you,

runways widened.

Magazines opened.

Young Black girls
looked at glossy pages
and finally saw
a reflection of their own brilliance.

Your legacy is not only the
photographs
frozen in time.

It is the doors
that will never close again.

It is the confidence
of every model who walks today
knowing the ground beneath her heels
was paved by courage.

So when fashion tells its story,
when history remembers its turning
points,

there will always be a chapter
written in elegance and strength

the moment
Veronica Webb stepped forward

and the world
followed her lead.

For Lil Mo
The Background Singer Who Became the Moment

They tried to keep you behind the
hook…
but your spirit kicked through
every chorus.

You weren't just a feature.
You were feeling.

The voice that made heartbreak sound
holy.
The tone that pulled rappers into
vulnerability
whether they liked it or not.

You were around
when love songs needed truth.
And you sang with the kind of cry
that made even liars pause.

But what they didn't always see
was the woman behind that ache.

The industry can be loud
and lonely at the same time.
And you walked through both
with your mic still steady.

They borrowed your voice
before they gave you your flowers.
They leaned on your emotion
before they acknowledged your strength.

Still
you kept showing up.

Through label politics.
Through public scrutiny.
Through love that didn't always love you
back.
Through the exhausting work
of proving you were more
than someone else's bridge.

You were small,
but your sound was loud enough
to echo through decades.

And that endurance?
That is sacred.

Because it takes a certain kind of woman
to be repeatedly underestimated
and still open her mouth to sing.

It takes healing
to turn pain into pitch control.
It takes resilience
to harmonize through heartbreak
and not let it harden you.

You didn't just sing about love.
You survived it.
You didn't just deliver emotion.
You carried it.

And every time your voice cracked just
enough
to feel human
you gave permission
for the rest of us
to feel too.

Mo,
you are not just nostalgia.
You are blueprint.

Of what it means
to endure quietly.
To outlast the moment.
To become the moment.

You are the proof
that being needed
is different from being seen
and that one day,
if you hold your note long enough,
the world will hear you fully.

Thank you
for every hook that healed us.
For every verse that held us.
For every season
you chose not to quit.

You are not background.

You are foundation.

And foundation
never fades.

For Spice
Where Honey Remembers Fire

She does not arrive as noise.
She arrives like a song the earth
already knows.

Before the stage, before the name,
there was a girl wrapped in sunlight
and salt air,
carrying a voice that sounded like
home
even before the world could hear it.

And when I hear her now,
it is not just music that reaches me.

It is something older.
Something that feels like hands on
my back
guiding me toward myself.

She makes remembering feel soft.

Like the ancestors are not distant,
but close enough to hum through
her,
close enough to dance again
in the body of a woman who refused
to forget them.

There is beauty in the way she holds
herself.
Not borrowed.
Not performed.

But grown.

Like fruit that ripens without asking
permission.
Like honey that does not rush its
sweetness.

She is not just fire.
She is what remains after the fire
learns how to love itself.

And in her, I see a woman
who did not have to break to
become powerful,
only to believe
that she already was.

And somewhere between her voice
and my spirit,
I feel something settle.

A quiet knowing.
A return.

That I come from something tender
and unafraid.
That I, too, am allowed to be both
soft and seen.

And heaven did not rush her into
becoming.
It watched her unfold
like something it had always
intended to keep.

For Wunmi Mosaku
The Woman Who Walks Through Shadows Unafraid

There is a quiet storm inside you.
Wunmi, you do not chase attention….
attention studies you.
Your eyes hold oceans.
Your stillness unsettles rooms.
You make vulnerability look like power.
In horror, you are not afraid.
In drama, you are not decorative.
In silence, you are not empty.
You feel ancient and modern at once …..
as if your spirit remembers something
the rest of us are still learning.
You remind us
that softness is not weakness.
That subtlety can shake foundations.
You don't dominate scenes.
You absorb them.
Transform them.
Leave them altered.
There is a sacred calm in you.
A knowing.
And that knowing lingers long after you exit frame.

For Aunjanue Ellis
Taylor The Woman Who Carries the Archive

You do not enter scenes.
You enter with history in your posture.
Aunjanue, your voice feels footnoted.
Researched. Rooted.
As if every word passed through
grandmothers before reaching your lips.
You do not rush emotion.
You hold it.
Let it simmer.
Let it speak in the silence.
There is something uncompromising about you.
You refuse to flatten yourself
for the comfort of casual audiences.
When you portray mothers,
they feel ancestral.
When you portray grief,
it feels inherited.
When you portray strength,
it is not spectacle
it is survival.
You remind us
that intelligence is sensual.
That dignity can be fierce.
That Black womanhood
is layered, not loud.
You are not here for performance.
You are here for preservation.
And the culture stands taller
because you insist on depth.

For Reagan Gomez
The Woman Who Felt Like Home

Reagan,

you were subtle impact.

You didn't need theatrics
to be felt.

On screens that shaped a generation,
you represented something steady.
Relatable.
Real.

There was intelligence in your
softness.
Strength in your stillness.
A groundedness that made your
characters breathe.

You weren't spectacle.

You were substance.

And beyond acting…
you evolved.

Writer.
Creator.
Architect of your own lane.

That transition matters.

Because it proves
you were never dependent on
visibility.

You were invested in voice.

Reagan,
thank you for representing Black girl
normalcy
without flattening it.

For showing that growth
can be quiet.
That ambition
can be balanced.
That motherhood and creativity
can coexist.

You may not shout legacy.

But you embody it.

And sometimes…
that's more powerful.

For Rosario Dawson
The Woman Who Moves Between Worlds

Rosario,

you've always felt borderless.

Film.
Indie.
Blockbuster.
Activism.
Politics.

You move between worlds
without losing center.

There's something grounded about
you…
even when the roles are larger than
life.

You bring texture to characters.
Not caricature.
Not convenience.

You don't just show up to be seen.
You show up to represent.

Afro-Latina presence.
Political awareness.
Art with backbone.

You have never been passive about
your platform.

And that matters.

Because visibility without
responsibility
is noise.

But you chose engagement.
Chose voice.
Chose participation in something
larger.

Rosario,
you embody expansion.

You prove that artistry
does not have to disconnect from
community.

That creativity
and consciousness
can coexist.

And that balance
is powerful.

For Alexis Fields
The Girl Who Grew Up With Us

Alexis,

you were the transition.

From child roles
to teenage depth,
you didn't disappear between eras…
you matured inside them.

You were part of the ecosystem
that made Black television feel continuous.
Familiar faces evolving in front of us.

There was something steady about you.
Never try-hard.
Never forced.

Just present.

And presence matters.

You existed in that sacred 90s–early 2000s window
where Black sitcoms weren't chasing relevance..
they were defining it.

You helped build that atmosphere.

And even if the spotlight shifted,
your imprint didn't.

You were part of our living room memories.
After-school reruns.
Theme songs we still hum.

Alexis,
thank you for growing with us
instead of fading from us.

That consistency?
That's legacy too.

For Yvette Wilson
The Woman Who Made Loud Sacred

Yvette,

Adele was not just comic relief.

She was truth in motion.

Volume with heart.
Shade with loyalty.
Timing that felt instinctual.

You didn't act like you were funny.

You knew you were.

And that confidence
shifted every room you stepped into.

You made sarcasm warm.
Made bluntness lovable.
Made bold Black woman energy
feel safe instead of threatening.

There was rhythm in your delivery.
Music in your pauses.
Precision in your punchlines.

And when you laughed…
we felt included.

You carried joy like armor.
Like someone who understood
that laughter is resistance.

Yvette,
you weren't side character.

You were anchor.

You gave us someone
who didn't shrink,
didn't soften herself
for approval.

And even after your passing,
the echo of your humor
still lives.

Because joy that real
doesn't vanish.

It lingers.

For Shar Jackson
The Girl Who Held Her Ground

Shar,

you were never fragile.

In an era that often reduced young
Black actresses
to tropes
the sidekick,
the loud friend,
the background energy

you held dimension.

On Moesha,
you weren't decoration.
You were balance.

Sarcasm with softness.
Edge with loyalty.
Confidence without cruelty.

There was something grounded
about you.
You felt real.
Like somebody's cousin.
Somebody's best friend.
Somebody who would tell you the
truth
even when it stung.

And when life tried to make your
personal story
into public spectacle
you did not unravel.

You stayed composed.
You stayed maternal.
You stayed intact.

That takes strength
the culture rarely acknowledges.

Shar,
you represent a generation
of Black women
who grew up in front of the world
and refused to let it define them.

You didn't chase spotlight.

You survived it.

And survival
with dignity
is its own form of grace.

For Naturi Naughton
The Woman Who Survived the Break and Became the Force

Naturi,

they tried to make you a footnote.

A replacement.
A former member.
A headline wrapped in teenage drama.

But you were never background.

From 3LW, you were presence.
Not just harmony…
foundation.

There was grit in your tone even then.
A depth that felt older than the
industry expected from you.

And when the narrative shifted…
when doors closed publicly,
when friendships fractured under
fluorescent lights…

you did not disappear.

You recalibrated.

That is power.

You stepped into acting
not as escape,
but as expansion.

You didn't just play characters.
You inhabited ambition.

Tasha St. Patrick wasn't accidental.
She was layered.
Strategic.
Feminine and formidable.

You gave us a Black woman
who could desire more
without apologizing for it.

You made vulnerability look
calculating.
You made motherhood look
commanding.
You made survival look like strategy.

And through it all…
you carried composure.

There is something groundbreaking
about a woman
who is publicly underestimated
and privately relentless.

You were dismissed.
And then you became undeniable.

That transition?
That is revolution.

Naturi,

you are not comeback story.

You are evolution.

You are proof
that rejection can refine.
That departure can redirect.
That early betrayal
does not define destiny.

You were always a force.

The industry just needed time
to catch up to your velocity.

And now?
They cannot ignore you.

The Ministry of Shade & Sweetness

"Where elegance meets edge….and every syllable lands"

For Mariah Huq
The Blueprint of Velvet & Vision

She did not walk in.
She arrived.

Not asking for space,
but carrying it
like something inherited.

With lace at the edge of her language
and power settled in her posture,
she moved like a woman
the room would adjust to.

Mariah is not just elegance.
She is lineage.

The echo of women
who built in silence,
who turned struggle into structure
and made vision visible
before it was believed.

She did not wait to be seen.
She became the lens
through which Black excellence
could witness itself
fully.

This is not surface.
This is strategy.

She speaks in layers.
Her silence holds court.
Every gesture
both branding and blessing.

Because when you build
what was never given to you,
you do not show up.
You design permanence.

They did not give her flowers.
So she learned the soil
and planted anyway.

A garden rooted in vision,
watered in resistance,
documented in bloom
so it could never be denied.

She did not just defy barriers.
She redefined access.

She walked into rooms
not built with her in mind
and left behind doorways.

That is not participation.
That is authorship.

Mariah,
you are not part of the cast.

You are the reason
the table exists.

You are not visibility.
You are vision
that refused to stay unseen.

This is not recognition.
This is revelation.

You are necessary.
You are remembered.
You are the blueprint.

For Quad Webb
A Toast to Every Version of Her

She did not just arrive.
She returned.

Again and again.
From rooms that misread her,
from stories told before she could
speak,
from seasons that would have
broken
a woman less fluent in becoming.

She does not discard her past.
She reclaims it.
Turns it into posture.
Wears it as presence.

She does not wear style.
She delivers it
like language that knows where it
belongs.

She has never arrived halfway.
Never spoken halfway.
Never chosen herself quietly.

There is fight in her softness.
Elegance in her edge.
The kind that does not perform
but survives.

She is the woman you remember
because she says what others
rehearse
and makes truth sound
worth repeating.

Her power is not in the image.
It is in the rebuild.
In the return
that does not ask to be accepted.

You do not meet Quad.
You experience
what it looks like
when a woman refuses
to be reduced.

And if you are paying attention,
you adjust.

Because she is not here
to be agreed with.
She is here
to be understood on her own terms.

She is every version
that survived the misunderstanding.
Every version
that chose herself
when it cost her.

This is not evolution.
This is resurrection
with memory intact.

So we do not just toast
who she is.
We honor every version
that refused to disappear.

She is not a moment.
She is continuity.

She is not what they said.
She is what remained.

She is necessary.
She is undeniable.
She is still becoming
and doing it out loud.

For NeNe Leakes
The Blueprint of Loud Truth and Louder Legacy

She did not disappear into grief.
She did not dissolve into silence.
She carried it.
And still showed up
with enough presence
to remind the world
that pain does not cancel power.
She is Atlanta's glitter and grit,
yes,
but she is also the woman
who learned how to survive loss
without letting it make her smaller.
They did not give her a script.
Because there is no script
for a woman who refuses
to be reduced to what she's been
through.
So she authored herself
in rhinestones and receipts,
in truth that didn't ask permission,
in moments that could not be edited
down
into something digestible.
She was called loud.
Because clarity
is offensive
to people who benefit from
distortion.
They said she was too much.
Because they had never witnessed a
woman
be exactly who she is
after life tried to take her apart
piece by piece.
And still
she chose visibility.
Not for applause.
Not for validation.

But because somewhere along the
way
she understood something sacred
that being seen fully
is not a privilege
it is a decision.
And she made it.
Over and over again.
Even when it hurt.
Even when it cost her.
Even when the world
only wanted the highlight
and not the history.

For Sheree Whitfield
The Art of Standing Still While They Talk

You do not rush.

You arrive.

Composure is not something
you perform.

It is something
you return to
when the room forgets
how to hold you correctly.

They called it attitude.

You called it boundaries
before the language
became popular.

You understood early
that presence
does not beg.

It waits.

And lets everything else
reveal itself.

There is a discipline
in the way you hold silence.

The way you let people speak
until they tell on themselves.

The way you choose
when to respond
and when to let the moment
stand on its own.

You never needed
to be the loudest.

Only the most certain.

There is sweetness in you
but it is not soft.

It is measured.

Given
with intention
not assumption.

And the shade

is never reckless.

It is placed.

Timed.

Delivered
like someone
who knows
exactly
what they are doing.

You made stillness
feel like power.

You made restraint
feel like control.

You made presence
feel like something
people had to adjust to
whether they were ready
or not.

And that is the thing
they could not quite name.

You are not reacting.

You are deciding.

For Kandi Burruss
The Woman Who Kept Making More

You feel like abundance with a pulse.

Not the loud kind.
The kind that keeps building
after the room has gone home,
turning heartbreak into harmony,
pressure into product,
vision into something we can hold.

You do not just create.
You multiply.

And that is different.

Because it takes a particular kind of
woman
to remain open enough to keep
giving
after the world has taken
so much for granted.

There is something holy
about the way you stayed fruitful.

People call it talent.
I see discipline.
I see a woman who kept choosing
herself
in rooms that wanted the fruit
without honoring the tree.

Your softness was never weakness.
It was stewardship.

Your success was never accidental.
It was earned
by every moment you kept going
when rest would have made more
sense,
by every time you refused
to let frustration poison the harvest.

And beneath all of that
is still a woman
who wanted to be met
with the same depth
she has spent a lifetime giving.

Not just the empire.
The woman inside it.

Not just the win.
The weight.

Kandi, you are not just successful.

You are sustaining.

You are what it looks like
when purpose keeps reproducing
itself
through a woman
who refused to let pain
make her barren.

For Mary Crosby
The Velvet Glitch in the Matrix

Mary does not live in your narrative.

She exists in her own.

Part First Lady,
part fever dream,

she moves through rooms
like she already knows
how they will end.

She sees what others miss,
says what others soften,

and wears presence
like something tailored
for impact.

Her silence is intentional.

Her distance
measured.

Her stillness
never empty.

There is something about her
that does not ask to be understood.

And does not need to be.

She confuses those
who rely on logic

because Mary moves
in instinct,
in timing,
in knowing
before knowing has language.

She does not explain.

She does not adjust.

She does not dilute.

She remains.

And beneath the elegance,
there is something else.

Discipline.

Control.

The kind of love
that does not announce itself
but shapes everything around it.

Not loud.
Not performative.

But present
in the way she stands,
in the way she protects,
in the way nothing
touches what is hers
without consequence.

For Phaedra Parks
The Southern Bell with Steel in Her Spine

She is the embodiment
of sweet tea and sudden silence.

Scripture carried in a smile.
Strategy concealed behind eyelashes
like a truth the room
was never trained to detect.

Because her power
does not announce itself.

It calibrates.

Measured.
Intentional.
Unmoved by the need
to be immediately understood.

She operates within a knowing

that gentleness
is not the absence of force

but its refinement.

There is archive in her restraint.

Generational intelligence
in the way she selects each word.

A lineage of women
who mastered survival
not through volume

but through precision.

She does not react.

She positions.

And in a culture
that confuses performance with
authority

she stands as correction

proof that composure
can still carry conviction

that grace
can function as strategy

that power
can remain intact
without spectacle.

I have studied women like her.

Observed how they carry
consequence
without display.

How they protect what matters
without requesting recognition.

So this is not admiration.

It is documentation.

Because women like her
do not simply participate in history

they stabilize it.

Reorient it.

Quietly enforce a standard
the room did not know
it had already failed to meet.

And when the moment passes

and noise forgets itself

what will remain

is not volume

but the precision
of a woman
who understood exactly
when to speak

and when to let silence
complete the argument.

For Marlo Hampton
The Woman Who Made Survival Look Like Style

Marlo,

before they learned to brand
struggle,
you were already wearing it
like it came stitched in silk…

Not borrowed.
Not softened.

You didn't become "hood rich"…
you redefined the currency.

Took what they called lack
and tailored it
into presence.

Every label
a declaration…

I made it out
and I will not shrink to prove it.

They saw flash…
missed the structure.

Didn't see the discipline
in your boundaries,
how you made "no"
feel like luxury.

They called you sharp
when you were precise.
Difficult
when you were unmovable.

But a woman who built herself
from survival
doesn't bend easily…
she chooses when to.

That's power
they don't know how to name.

You didn't enter rooms
to be accepted…
you changed the temperature.

Fashion wasn't escape.
It was language.

Every look…
a sentence.
Every silence…
a chapter they couldn't read.

And while they debated your edges,
you were building something
quieter…

two boys
learning safety
from a woman
who had to invent it.

That's legacy.

Not the spectacle…
the stability.

Marlo,

you are not the exception.

You are the blueprint
of a woman
who refused to apologize
for becoming.

And that…
is what they never got right.

For Candace Dillard Bassett
In Full Bloom, With a Razor in Her Smile

In the land of milk and honey,
she walked in
pearl-strung spine,
a voice trained to cut clean.

A daughter of decorum and dream,
where prep schools and pageants
taught posture before presence,
before the fire she learned
to tuck beneath each syllable.

She was not just raised.

She was refined.

Not soft, but precise.
Not spoiled, but disciplined
in the art of proving brilliance
in rooms that already questioned it.

A nepo baby, they called her,
as if inheritance erases effort,
as if access replaces sharpening.

As if softness cannot carry edge
when raised by women
who expect both.

Candace,

with the tongue of a scholar
and the stillness of someone
who has learned
when to strike
and when to let silence
do the work,

you are not for the comfortable.

You are for those who understand
that beauty, unguarded,
is currency,

but beauty, controlled,
is strategy.

And I see you.

Not just the woman they call too
much,
but the one they could not outpace,
could not out-speak,
could not outgrow.

I see the discipline beneath the
delivery.
The intention beneath the tone.
The restraint beneath the reaction.

I see all of us
who learned to be fully formed
in a world that prefers us
unfinished.

So here are your flowers, Candace.

Not as permission to bloom,
but as recognition
that you already did.

With edge intact.
With intellect unsoftened.
With elegance
that never asked
to be misunderstood.

For Stacey Rush
She don't raise her voice...she adjusts the room.

She walks in with the poise of a
Sunday prayer
and the polish of a deal closed
before the cameras ever roll.

A saleswoman turned sovereign,
silk voice resting easy on bone china,
delivering grace without effort,

her cadence selling more than
products.

She sells presence.

Stacey doesn't raise her voice.

She adjusts the room.

QVC taught her persuasion,
but Potomac revealed her power,

where her restraint sharpened,
where her silence started speaking,

where elegance stopped asking
to be noticed.

Not everyone understands
the language of a woman
who never needs to break.

She bends time with a raised brow,
shifts energy with a glance,

sits at tables
where class is not performed
but inherited
through posture,
through knowing.

Some will call her composed.

Too calculated.

That is the language
of the unprepared.

Stacey Rush did not arrive
to be liked.

She arrived to be remembered.

To remind you
that class, when embodied,
does not need explanation.

She is not part of the story.

She is the standard.

For Angela Oakley
The woman who rose without flinching

You were never just a housewife…
you were the hearth, the pillar, the flame.
You stitched legacy into silence,
held composure like prayer,
while winds whispered stories meant to undo you.
Chicago carved your bones,
but you crowned yourself in a mirror
that never lied.
Self-made in the truest tongue…
you gathered gold from broken glass
and wore resilience like red velvet.
The world watched your grace…
but I saw your spine.
The nights you held your breath
so your children wouldn't hear the cracking.
The mornings you laced power
between your lashes and your quiet.
And me…
a little Black boy from the same soil,
watching you carry poise in places
where most would've folded.
You didn't just survive;
you taught survival how to blossom.
Angela, you are scripture in stilettos,
a psalm for the self-built,
the still-standing.
This is not just a poem…
it's an offering.
A soft bouquet for the woman
who walked through fire
and still smelled like honey.

For the Grande Dame
(Karen Huger), from a Son of the Soil

You walked in, and time
paused
like even the air understood
it needed to behave.

Grand Dame, they call you
but I call you proof

that legacy can have hips,
that grace can carry a blade,
that a woman's name can become
her own inheritance

even when the world tries
to write footnotes where crowns belong.

You speak with the memory
of the South
and the posture of Paris

but I see something deeper

I see a woman
who learned how to hold herself together
when the room stopped clapping

who did not collapse
when the spotlight turned sharp

who understood that dignity
is not the absence of mistake
but the decision
to remain whole through it

Hair like a sermon
Smile like Sunday

but even sermons have valleys
and Sundays don't come
without a week behind them

You did not ask for a seat
at the table

You became the table
and then made it something
no one could ignore

even when they tried
to question the wood
the weight
the foundation

From the South Side to Surrey County
I saw myself in your climb

not just in your rise
but in your refusal

in the way you did not shrink
even when the room expected you to fold

even when the world
tried to reduce you
to a moment

as if a woman could be summarized
by a single misstep

as if elegance
had no right to be human

Karen

this is from a little Black boy
who watched women like you

hold everything together
with press-ons and prayer
and never call it strength

who watched you
stand in your name
even when it was being called into question

You taught me
that royalty is not inherited

It is chosen

and choosing it
means standing

not just when it's easy
not just when it's celebrated

but when it's examined
misunderstood
and still yours to carry

And you carried it

fully
loudly
without asking
if you were allowed

And that

that is why you are the Grand Dame

For Drew Sidora
The Woman Who Stayed Anyway

Drew,

you came from the South Side of
Chicago,
where softness wears armor
and presence is learned like prayer.

You carried that
through Hollywood,

a place that edits women
like scripts
and calls it destiny.

But you did not arrive polished.

You arrived
mid-sentence.

Still translating yourself
between who you were
and who they rehearsed you to be.

Then Atlanta.

A louder room.
A sharper mirror.
A stage that does not whisper
when it decides who you are.

And still,

you stood in it.

Not always landing like applause.
Sometimes like a skipped beat.
Sometimes like a line delivered
too early for the room.

But still…

you stayed.

Because some women
move like marble.

Unquestioned.
Untouched.

But you…

you move like water
learning the shape of every room
while still refusing to disappear.

From Chicago
to Hollywood
to Atlanta,

you have been
a sentence still becoming.

Not finished.
Not flawless.
But spoken
out loud.

And in a world
that trims women
into silence,

you let the process breathe.

And breath,

held long enough,

becomes presence.

For Eva Marcille
The Confidence She Carried

You didn't just walk into the room.
You made presence feel necessary.

I was a little Black boy from Chicago
watching you move like beauty
did not require permission,
only ownership.

And something in me
stood up.

Because you never asked to be
chosen.
You arrived already decided.

Even in your wildness
there was alignment.

Not chaos.
Not confusion.

Just a woman
refusing to edit her becoming
for comfort.

They called it attitude.

I recognized sovereignty.

The kind that doesn't raise its voice,
just its standard.

Eva,

your confidence felt ancestral.

Like somewhere before cameras,
before casting calls,
a lineage of women
had already agreed
you would not shrink.

There was something in your
stillness.

Sharp.
Intentional.

Like even your silence
knew exactly where it stood.

You weren't just modeling clothes.

You were modeling possession.

What it looks like
when a woman stands in her body
like it belongs to her.

Fully.

And I carried that.

Still do.

Because you showed me
that beauty is not softness alone.

It is structure.
It is boundary.
It is knowing
you are the standard
even when the room
hasn't caught up yet.

So no,

you weren't just a contestant.

You were curriculum.

A lesson in presence
I didn't know I was studying
but never forgot.

For Dr. Heavenly Kimes
She Bit Because She Cared

Your voice cuts clean.

But that is how protectors speak.

You do not raise your volume without
reason.

You raise it
when something you love
is at risk of being mishandled.

They call you loud.

Because they do not recognize
urgency
when it comes from a woman
who refuses to let things break quietly.

You clap back
because you were never built
to bow.

And beneath all of it

there is order.

Tradition.
Discipline.
A woman rooted in more than
credentials.

You are scripture and surgery.

Faith in one hand.
Precision in the other.

You navigate rooms
where ego speaks first
and still find a way
to advocate for minds,
for healing,
for the parts of people
no one films.

You carry politics
without dropping your practice.

Run a business,

a household,
a legacy

and still show up
to screens across the country
with truth in your mouth
like medicine.

You built a family,
a practice,
and a voice

that does not wait
to be validated.

There is a heart behind the heat.

A prayer behind the punchline.

A knowing
behind every word
people try to dismiss too quickly.

They say messy.

Because layered
requires attention.

And those of us who understand

know your name is not just Heavenly.

It is intention.

It is structure.

It is a woman
who refuses to separate
grace from grit.

I see you.

Not as noise.

But as necessity.

You are proof
that strength does not need softness
to be sacred.

For Eboni K. Williams
She Who Spoke Truth in a White Room

You didn't just enter.

You arrived like verdict.

An Ivy-shaped presence
draped in Harlem's discipline
and undeniable command,

you made it clear
that grace and justice
could occupy the same space

even when the room
was built to resist both.

You turned silence into strategy.

Did not flinch
when microaggressions disguised
themselves
as casual conversation.

You brought your grandmother's
wisdom
and your ancestors' expectations
into a space
that had never been required
to hold either.

Eboni, you were not there to
entertain.

You were the interruption.

Composure wrapped in couture,
a woman who understood
that presence alone
could shift the terms of engagement.

You were never a subplot.

You were the question
they did not want to answer.

For Garcelle Beauvais
Hollywood Doesn't Make Stars Like You Anymore

Before Beverly Hills,
you were already gold.

Not plated.
Not polished.

Proven.

A first of many,
moving through rooms
that were not designed
to recognize you

and still choosing
to be unmistakable.

Your smile does not soften the
room.

It steadies it.

Your laughter does not entertain.

It liberates.

You understood something early:

visibility is not the same
as belonging.

And still,
you stayed.

Frame by frame,
role by role,

you built a presence
that could not be edited out
or reduced to supporting.

You walked into those scenes
like the camera
had something to learn from you.

Mother.

Maven.

Mover.

Not performance.

Position.

You held your ground
like someone who has been
the only Black face in the room
too many times
to confuse discomfort
with danger.

Garcelle,

you did not make glamour smaller
to fit the moment.

You made it honest.

And in doing so,

you gave other women
a language for their own presence
before they ever had the room
to use it.

"I am not alone in this orbit."

That is what your existence says
without asking permission.

And that

is how legacy is built:

not by arrival,

but by endurance
that refuses
to disappear.

For Bozoma Saint John
The Boardroom's Butterfly

You did not enter the room.

You altered its temperature.

What was once sterile
learned how to breathe
when you spoke.

They called it presence.

But presence is too small a word
for a woman who turns institutions
into something that has to feel her.

You walked in carrying more than title.

You carried lineage
draped in color.

History
styled in intention.

A memory of somewhere deeper
than corporate glass could hold.

Your hair did not just make statements.

It archived them.

Your clothes did not ask permission.

They testified.

And somewhere between strategy and spirit
you taught them

that brilliance does not have to translate
itself
to be understood.

It can arrive whole
and let the room adjust.

You are not contradiction.

You are convergence.

Where Sankofa meets stock options.

Where rhythm meets revenue.

Where culture refuses
to be separated
from power.

Boz,

you did not disrupt the algorithm.

You rewrote what it rewards.

Because before you
they mistook assimilation for excellence.

After you

they had to reckon with the fact
that authenticity performs better
when it is not diluted.

And I watched that.

I watched you sit in rooms
that were never designed
to hold the fullness of you

and still expand them
until they had no choice.

This is not style.

This is architecture.

The kind that builds new ceilings
and then erases them.

So when you walk in now

it is not entrance.

It is precedent.

And somewhere
a young Black girl
is learning

that she does not have to shrink
to be strategic

that she can be vivid
and still be valued

that she can be all the way herself
and still own the room.

That is your legacy.

Not just that you were seen.

But that because you were

others no longer have to ask
if they can be.

For Kenya Moore
Gone With the Wind, Still Here With Grace

You did not spin for them.

You spun for the girl
who learned early
that silence can swallow a name
if you don't make it echo.

And look at you now

echo turned empire.

They tried to name you storm.

But storms do not hold this much
precision.

You are not chaos.
You are calibration.

Every word measured.
Every glance intentional.
Every exit
a lesson in timing.

They called you villain.

But villains do not build themselves
this deliberately.

They do not turn pain
into posture.

They do not take rejection
and refine it
until it looks like arrival.

I saw you.

Not just the twirl
but the discipline behind it.

The way you made elegance
out of endurance.

The way you wore composure
like armor
lined in silk.

You taught us something
they still refuse to admit

that a woman can be both
mirror and fire

reflecting truth
while burning illusion.

And yes

you stood alone.

But solitude, on you,
never looked like absence.

It looked like authorship.

Like a woman
refusing to be edited
by people who never
understood the assignment.

So let me say it correctly

You were never "too much."

You were exact.

Exact in a world
that survives on dilution.

Exact in a room
that profits off confusion.

And that crown?

It was never given.

It recognized you.

This is not nostalgia.

This is record.

Because long after the noise
forgets itself

your name will still read
like intention

like survival
refined into elegance

like a woman
who did not just endure the wind

but learned how to move through it
without ever losing
her center.

For Lesa Milan
The Woman Who Built Quietly

Lesa,

you don't perform power.
You accumulate it.

There is something disciplined about you.
Measured. Strategic. Observant.

You walk into rooms like a woman
who has already assessed them.

Fashion wasn't vanity for you.
It was leverage.
It was positioning.
It was proof that aesthetics can fund autonomy.

You built a brand while cameras rolled.
You mothered without collapsing.
You defended yourself without theatrics.

There is restraint in your strength.

And that restraint is often misunderstood
as softness.

But softness is not weakness.
It's control.

You do not waste words.
You do not move impulsively.
You choose your alliances carefully.

Lesa,
you represent the Black woman
who knows that being underestimated
is sometimes an advantage.

You didn't scream dominance.

You engineered it.

And that is far more dangerous.

For Cynthia Bailey
The Beauty That Learned How to Breathe Without Apology

She was never just a face.
That was the doorway they chose, not the house she built.

Long before the cameras, and long after the applause learned her name, she was practicing stillness. The kind that does not beg to be noticed, only honored.

God did not rush her.
He shaped her in quiet rooms where mirrors could not affirm her, and still she learned how to stand.

They called it beauty because they did not have language for grace that refuses to perform. They called it softness because they could not recognize discipline when it is dressed in ease.

But she knew.

She knew what it meant to be chosen for the outside and still cultivate an interior no camera could capture. She knew what it meant to stay open in rooms that only understood armor.

There is a sacred patience woven through her story. Not the patience of waiting, but the patience of becoming without breaking.

She loved. She learned. She let go.
And somehow, she remained whole.

That is not beauty.
That is anointing.

Because not every woman is called to be loud. Some are called to hold frequency, to enter a room and remind everything in it that grace still exists.

She is that reminder.

A woman who made elegance feel like truth. Who made presence feel like prayer. Who made becoming look effortless when it was anything but.

And even now, she does not ask to be seen correctly. She simply is.

And in that, she becomes not just a woman to admire, but a woman to study.

A living scripture written in poise, refined by time, and sealed in quiet power.

And heaven, without raising its voice, called her beautiful long before the world caught up.

Katie Rost
The Woman Who Was Too Honest for the Room

Katie,

you were never chaotic.

You were unfiltered in a room
that survives on performance.

From the moment you appeared,
there was something different about
you.
Soft-spoken but sharp.
Gentle but observant.

You didn't argue loudly.
You dismantled quietly.

And that unsettled people.

Because truth delivered calmly
is harder to deflect.

You were biracial in a cast navigating
Blackness.
Jewish in a franchise built on image.
Open about pain in a space that edits
vulnerability.

You didn't perform stability.
You didn't fake polish.

You let the cracks show.

And instead of protecting you,
the room tried to label you.

But here's the truth:

You were ahead of the emotional
conversation.

You spoke about identity
before it was comfortable.
About mental health
before it was marketable.
About motherhood and custody
battles
without pretending to be perfect.

That kind of transparency
is threatening.

Katie,
you were not unstable.

You were exposed.

And exposure without protection
looks messy to people
who are hiding.

There is something sacred
about a woman
who refuses to fake composure
for applause.

You were fragile and fearless at once.
Raw and reflective.

You didn't stay long in the spotlight.

But you left imprint.

Because sometimes the woman
who cannot fully conform to the
machine
is the most human one in it.

And humanity…
real, complicated, imperfect
humanity…
is always more revolutionary
than polish.

You were never too much.

You were simply unwilling
to lie.

And that matters.

For Claudia Jordan
The Unedited Frame

Before they learned your name,
they learned your face..
and thought that was enough.

But you were never just
a still image.

You were motion.
Voice.
Opinion wrapped in beauty
they didn't know how to hold.

They tried to frame you..
pose you into silence,
edit you into something easier to
digest.

But you refused.

You spoke.
Even when it cost you rooms.
Even when the air shifted
because your truth entered it.

Claudia…

you are the kind of woman
they misunderstand first
and respect later.

Because you don't perform
palatability.
You don't shrink your voice
to stay invited.

You walk in already knowing…
you are the conversation.

Not decoration.

And let's be clear…

your shade was never accidental.
It was tailored.
Measured like couture.
Delivered with precision
that only a woman who sees clearly
can possess.

Not cruelty…

but clarity with teeth.

The kind that exposes without
raising its voice.
The kind that makes truth
feel like a mirror
people weren't ready to look into.

You belong in the Ministry of Shade
not because you throw it…
but because you understand
its language.

Its timing.
Its purpose.

You are proof
that beauty can think,
can challenge,
can disrupt without asking
permission.

And that unsettles people
who only know how to receive
women
in pieces.

But you came whole.

Unapologetic.
Unedited.

And that is where your power lives.

Not in being liked..
but in being **undeniably real**.

You didn't just exist in the spotlight.

You learned how to stand in it
without letting it rewrite you.

And for that,

we don't just see you
as the image they tried to capture…

we see you
as the woman
who refused to be reduced to it.

The Ones Who Spoke in Frequencies

"The Visionaries Who Broke Form and Became Freedom"

For Solange
Who Taught Us to Sculpt Stillness

You didn't need to shout.
Your silence carried more gravity
than most anthems.

Solange,
you are the pause that teaches.
The breath between movements.
The space that makes the sound
sacred.

You didn't just sing..
you curated.
Pain, softness, disruption.
Braids, bass lines, broken systems.
You turned all of it into a canvas.

You taught us that healing is
layered..
sometimes a ritual,
sometimes a rage,
sometimes just a rhythm you repeat
until it becomes whole.

You gave us permission to cry in
sunlight.
To wear white and still be angry.
To honor our grandmothers with
our style
and our truth.

You made Black girl magic into
museum work.
And every girl who ever felt unseen
found herself in the quiet of your
choreography.

You didn't crave the moment.
You became the moment
we didn't know we needed.
The one that sits in the chest
long after the song is over.

You are not a pop star.
You are a portal.
A sound bath.
A blueprint for softness with
boundaries.

And every time you braid your
hair…
another veil lifts.
Another ancestral language is spoken
without a single word.

You taught us that revolution
can look like stillness.
That rage can be held
without being loud.

You walk into rooms
like you've already blessed them.
And maybe you have.

For Doja Cat
Uncontainable Divine Fem

Doja,

you were never confusion.

You were combustion.

They called you strange
because they could not predict you.
They called you chaotic
because they could not control you.

But I saw precision.

A mind that bends genre
without asking permission.
Pop in one hand.
Rap in the other.
Satire tucked behind your teeth.

You don't chase acceptance.
You dare the room to adjust.

When you shaved your head,
you stripped away expectation
and stood there anyway
unapologetic, unornamented,
unowned.

That was power.

You made weird sacred.
You made internet-born Black girls
visible.
You made contradiction feel
intentional.

Soft and serrated.
Alien and ancestral.
Playful and surgical.

The industry loves a formula.

You are the glitch.

They try to decode you,
reduce you,
headline you.

But innovation is always
misunderstood
before it is revered.

You did not come to be digestible.

You came to expand what is allowed.

And that is not chaos.

That is courage.

Doja,

you are not too much.

You are uncontainable.

For Chloe Bailey X Halle Bailey
Two Voices, One Inheritance

Before the world called it harmony,
it was survival.
Two girls
learning how to hold sound
without dropping themselves inside of
it.

You can hear it if you listen right
not just the notes,
but the discipline it took
to not lose your individual breath
inside a shared one.

Because being seen together
is not the same
as being known separately.
And y'all learned that early.
Chloe

you carry the fire.
Not loud for attention,
but loud because silence
never felt honest in your body.

You move like a voice
that refuses to be contained
by expectation.
And sometimes they mistake that for
too much
but too much
is just another word
for something
they don't know how to hold.

Halle
you carry the water.
Not quiet out of fear,
but quiet because your depth
doesn't need to announce itself.
You move like something
that understands timing.
And they mistake that for softness
but softness

is just another form
of control.
Together
you are tension
that learned how to sing.

Not identical.
Not interchangeable.

But aligned
in a way
that doesn't erase difference
it honors it.
Because the truth is
not every duo survives
what the world projects onto them.
Comparison.
Division.
The need to choose.

But y'all didn't split.
You expanded.
You allowed yourselves
to become fully separate
without breaking the bond
that made you recognizable together.
And that's rare.
That's gospel.

Because what you represent
is not perfection
it's permission.
For two things to exist at once
power
and softness
visibility
and restraint
independence
and loyalty

You didn't just sing together.
You showed what it looks like
to grow
without abandoning
where you came from.

You are not one voice divided
you are two truths
that learned how to stand
next to each other
without shrinking
or competing
for space.

For Cree Summers
the Wild Laugh of Legacy

You weren't just a voice…
you were a vibration.
A song that slipped through Saturday mornings
and cradled the softest parts of our growing hearts.
We didn't know, not fully,
that your chords were braided with spirit…
with rebellion wrapped in velvet,
with medicine disguised as mischief.
You made the weird kids holy.
You made the awkward ones glow.
You gave soul to cartoons,
and gave cartoons to our soul.
Your voice didn't just speak…it cast spells.
Across screens, across time,
into bedrooms where Black children
were building dreams from hand-me-downs and hope.
We followed your sound like a map.
It led us to freedom.
It reminded us we didn't have to be loud to be powerful,
but it sure felt good when we were.
Cree,
you've always been more than Summer…
you were our Spring.
The blooming. The unfurling.
The proof that softness doesn't shrink
and oddness is divine.
So this love letter is loud,
a cartoon of gratitude and grace.
You shaped us without ever preaching.
You raised us without ever aging.
And we still hear you.
In every fierce whisper.
In every unshamed laugh.
In every child who refuses to be silenced.
Thank you for showing us
that the magic was never make-believe…
it was always your voice.

For Myha'la
The Woman Who Refused to Dilute

Myha'la,
you don't enter rooms to be liked.
You enter them to be undeniable.
There is something electric about
your presence
not loud,
not forced,
but sharp.

Like a woman who understands
that precision cuts deeper than
volume.
On screens that often demand
Black women to soften,
to round their edges,
to become palatable
you did the opposite.

You leaned in.
Into the discomfort.
Into the ambition.
Into the parts of womanhood
that are not always easy to celebrate.
You played hunger without apology.
You embodied drive without shame.
You let complexity live
without trying to make it pretty.

And that unsettled people.
Because they are used to seeing
Black women
as caretakers,
as background,
as emotional anchors for everyone
else.
But you?
You centered yourself.
You showed what it looks like
when a Black woman chooses
herself
in a world that rarely chooses her
first.

There is courage in that.
Not the kind that shouts
the kind that stays steady
when the room doesn't know how to
receive you.

Myha'la,
you represent a generation
that is no longer asking for
permission
to take up space.
You are ambition without apology.
You are edge without dilution.
You are proof
that complexity is not a flaw
it is depth.
And depth
cannot be ignored.
You didn't come to be comfortable.
You came to be real.
And real
always leaves a mark.

For Left Eye
She Saw, So I Could See

When I was young,
I didn't know the word for vision.
I just knew there was this woman…
with fire on her tongue
and planets in her pupils.

She didn't move like the others.
She moved like her thoughts were already songs,
like her questions had choreography,
like truth didn't need approval,
just volume.

Left Eye didn't teach me to be loud.
She taught me how to listen to my chaos.
How to wear flame on my fingertips
and call it clarity.
How to make mirrors nervous.

I used to draw on my sneakers,
thinking maybe if I colored them wild enough,
I'd run into the future she came from.

She made me ask:
what if soft could still be sharp?
What if being strange was the first step toward being seen?
What if vision wasn't something you found…
but something you uncovered inside your own skin?

Left Eye didn't just inspire me.
She rewired me.
She taught me that weird wasn't a phase…
it was a frequency.
And I've been vibrating different ever since.

So if you ever catch me dancing off-beat,
or talking like my dreams are already documentaries…
just know it's her.
Still flickering.
Still showing me how to see.

For Janelle
Who Time-Traveled in Tuxedos

You didn't just arrive...
you transmitted.
A glitch in the system.
A blessing in disguise.
A quiet defiance cloaked in couture.

Janelle,
you are the code and the crash.
The ancestor and the algorithm.
The conductor of a frequency
that made gender, time, and genre
bend at the knee.

You made tuxedos look like truth.
Patent leather like protest.
You danced like you'd memorized
the stars...
like they whispered choreography
into your spine.

You weren't trying to blend in.
You were blueprinting the future...
in heels, in harmony, in hardware.

You gave us rhythm
and resistance.
You gave us sci-fi that felt ancestral.
Feminine that felt like armor.
Queerness that wasn't theory...
it was theater.

You weren't just singing.
You were spelling.
Rewriting the sonic DNA
of a generation
too sacred to be small.

You taught me that to be "too
much"
is to be perfectly aligned
in a world that cannot hold
multitudes.

You made it safe
for us to moonwalk past binaries,
to kiss our reflection
without needing an apology.

You're what happens
when soul meets circuitry.
When voice meets vessel.
When truth refuses to die quietly.

You wore suits like skin.
And later...
you wore skin like sovereignty.

You are the glitch in the machine
that made the world
wake up.

For Khia
The One Who Answered to No One

The One Who Answered to No One

Before authenticity became a
currency,
you were already a consequence.

Unfiltered.
Unmoved.
Unapologetic.

You said what you said
and let the room wrestle with it.

Don't Trust No N****
was not just a record
it was a sermon.

Not to tear men down
but to sharpen discernment
to name the difference
between presence and pretense.

A warning dressed in rhythm.
A boundary that traveled borders.
A truth that echoed far beyond the
block
into rooms that pretended not to
hear it
but carried it anyway.

They called you loud
because your clarity disrupted
comfort.
Called you raw
because you refused to dilute.

So they tried to frame you
as a moment
something to outgrow
something to dismiss.

But truth does not expire.

It lingers.
It circulates.
It returns.

And here you are

Still quoted.
Still referenced.
Still felt.

Not because they agreed
but because they recognized
themselves in it.

You were never a moment.

You were a warning.
A mirror.
A refusal.

A woman who chose clarity
over approval.

And that

is what lasts.

For Vanessa Williams
The Crown They Could Not Take

Before the applause returned,
before the standing ovations
and the golden lights of Broadway

there was a storm.

A crown placed gently on your head,
then snatched away
by hands afraid of your brilliance.

But Vanessa

they misunderstood something
sacred.

Crowns made by people
can be taken.

But the crown
woven from resilience
cannot be removed.

When the world whispered doubt,
you answered with melody.

When they tried to write your
ending,
you began a new verse.

And suddenly your voice
rose like sunrise over silence

a reminder
that destiny does not belong
to the loudest critics,

but to the woman
who refuses to stop singing.

Now history remembers
not the scandal,

but the triumph.

Not the fall,

but the flight.

Because the truth is simple

they never really took your crown.

They only revealed
how powerful you were
without it.

For Vanessa Estelle Williams
The Woman of Unshakable Fire

There are women
who enter a room quietly.

And there are women
whose presence
changes the temperature of the air.

Vanessa Estelle Williams
you have always been the latter.

A woman whose voice
carries both velvet and steel,
whose spirit walks
with the certainty
of someone who knows
exactly who she is.

The world first met your fire
in characters who spoke boldly,
who stood their ground
when the room grew uncomfortable.

Women who refused
to shrink themselves
to make others feel tall.

Maxine was not just a role
she was a mirror
for every woman
who has ever been called
"too strong,"
"too outspoken,"
"too much."

But you showed us something sacred

that strength
is not a flaw.

It is a legacy.

And behind the fierce intelligence,
behind the commanding presence
that made audiences lean forward
in their seats

there has always been
a deeper brilliance.

A woman who understands
that power
is not about domination.

It is about knowing your worth
so clearly
that the world must adjust itself
to your truth.

Vanessa,
your career has never been
about noise.

It has been about impact.

The kind that lingers
long after the scene ends.

The kind that reminds young women
watching from living rooms and bedrooms
that their voice
does not need permission.

Because when you stand in a role,
when you speak a line,
when you carry a character

you are teaching something timeless:

That confidence
is not arrogance.

That intelligence
is not intimidation.

And that a woman
who stands firmly in herself
is not too much.

She is exactly enough.

And somewhere tonight
another young girl
is watching you on a screen
learning quietly

how to walk into the world
with her head high
and her spirit unshaken.

Because women like you
do more than act.

They leave behind
a blueprint of courage.

And your name

Vanessa Estelle Williams

will always carry the echo
of a woman
who showed us all
what strength looks like
when it wears grace.

For Aaliyah
The Whisper That Could Fly

You moved like silk in slow wind…
always just ahead of the time that tried to claim you.
Not loud,
but unforgettable.
Not boastful,
but built from brilliance.

Aaliyah,
you were the hush that made heads turn.
The softness that slipped through expectations
and turned every beat into a prayer for more.
You taught us that mystery
is a form of protection…
that when you carry the divine,
you don't need to explain it.

You danced like God had trusted you with gravity
and you chose to give it back.
And in your absence,
we felt the weight of what it means
to lose someone who carried light in their bones.

You didn't just belong to a moment.
You became the blueprint
for women who would later float,
for boys like me
who learned that softness can be sacred,
and that gone too soon
doesn't mean forgotten.

You are still here,
still whispered in every falsetto,
still gliding in the corner of every room
where grace chooses to land.

For Missy Elliot
The Blueprint of Boundless

You didn't walk through doors.
You blasted them off the hinges.
Beat by beat.
Word by word.
Wig by wig.

Missy,
you made **avant-garde** accessible.
Made weird fashionable.
Made feminine formless.
You walked into a male-drenched genre
and turned the whole studio into your **playground.**

You didn't just rap.
You constructed worlds.
Afrofuturist.
Sensual.
Silly.
Sharp.
And **brilliant** beyond metric.

You were a music video before we even knew what the hell we were looking at.
A sonic fingerprint.
A full-bodied YES to being different without explanation.

Your voice was a spell.
Your cadence was coded.
You weren't trying to be digestible…
you were becoming impossible to replicate.

And in that?
You birthed an entire generation
of creatives who no longer ask permission
to be **too much.**

You are every child who beatboxed in their bedroom mirror.
Every girl who dared to wear it backwards.
Every Black kid who made art from the edge.

You made it **cool to be cosmic.**
And we are still catching up to your vibration.

For Patina Miller
To the Woman Who Carried Fire Like It Was Light

You didn't just play Raq.
You *became* the scripture.
A woman with war in her walk,
and lullabies in her eyes
that only the worthy could hear.
When you spoke,
it felt like a grandmother's warning
wrapped in a big sister's dare.
Like a woman who's loved too hard,
bled too long,
but never once broke
in front of the men who wanted her
to.
And off-screen?
You're the rare kind…
the kind whose voice holds theatre
and thunder,
who steps into every stage like she's
been sent,
not cast.
You sing like the spirit remembers
you.
You move like your bones got
rhythm
from the ones who danced before
chains,
before scripts,
before anyone dared to name a Black
woman *divine.*
I've seen you hold power
like it's perfume…
undeniable but never loud.
Like you've learned the trick
of being both **miracle** and **muscle.**
You make me believe in grace with
backbone.
In softness with a blade.
In women who don't ask the world
to see them…
they *turn the lights on themselves.*

This is not just a love letter.
It's a *thank you*
from every soul who saw you
and remembered that they, too,
could lead.
Could love.
Could survive.
You are every note in the storm.
And the silence after.
And the reason we still watch
even when the credits roll.

For Kimberly Elise
The Woman Who Carries Truth

Some actresses perform.

You reveal.

Kimberly Elise,

your presence
has never been a character.

It is a pulse.

When you appear,
the room quiets.

Not out of politeness.

Out of recognition.

Because we are not watching.

We are witnessing.

You have carried women
whose pain was heavy,
whose hope was fragile,
whose strength
was built in places
no one should have to survive.

And you never softened them.

You honored them.

Your beauty was never loud.

It did not need to be.

It moves like light.
Steady.
Unforced.
Certain.

Because the greatest artists
do not chase attention.

They hold mirrors.

And through you,
we have seen ourselves.

Strength
that trembles.

Strength
that breaks.

And still

stands.

Your legacy
is not performance.

It is truth
that refused
to be hidden.

For Malinda Williams
The Quiet Strength of Grace

Some women enter a room
like thunder.

But you

you arrive like sunlight.

Soft, steady,
the kind of warmth
that fills the space
before anyone notices.

Malinda Williams,
your beauty has never been loud.

It is the kind
that whispers confidence
without needing applause.

The kind
that teaches grace
simply by existing.

The world met you
through stories
through characters
who carried tenderness
in a world that often rewards
hardness.

And when you gave life to Bird,
you gave us something rare:

a woman learning
that strength
does not mean silence.

A woman discovering
that love
must begin with herself.

Because sometimes
the most powerful journey
is not conquering the world

it is learning
how to heal your own heart.

And through every role,
every quiet moment

where your eyes spoke
before the script ever could,

you reminded us
that vulnerability
is not weakness.

It is courage.

Your presence
has always carried
a certain peace.

The kind that says
a woman can be gentle
and still unbreakable.

The kind that reminds young girls
watching from living rooms

that beauty
is not only in appearance

it is in spirit,
in resilience,
in the quiet decision
to keep choosing joy.

Malinda Williams,

your legacy is not only
the characters you portrayed.

It is the feeling
you leave behind.

A reminder
that grace
is a form of strength.

And strength
can look like a woman
walking through life
with softness in her heart
and dignity in her stride.

And that kind of beauty

never fades.

For Wendy Williams
She Asked the Question Nobody Else Would

Before the fall,
before the freeze-frames,
before the world learned how cruel
curiosity can be....
there was a woman with a
microphone
and no fear of the air.
Wendy did not whisper.
She carved space in it.
She was loud
because the industry was louder.
She was sharp
because the room was full of dull
lies.
They called her messy.
But messy is just what truth looks
like
when it refuses to be dressed
politely.
She asked the questions
everybody else rehearsed around.
She held celebrities in one hand
and accountability in the other.
And she did it in heels.
But beneath the wigs
and the side-eye
and the "How you doin'?"....
there was a woman
who built an empire
with nothing but nerve and knowing.
She taught us that a Black woman
does not have to be soft
to be successful.
She can be brash.
She can be bold.
She can be unliked
and still undeniable.
And when the lights dimmed
and the stage grew quiet,
we were forced to see
how lonely it can be
to carry a culture
on your tongue.

Wendy,
you were never just tea.
You were temperature.
You changed it.
This is not pity.
This is reverence.
Because before podcasts,
before timelines,
before everybody had an opinion...
there was you.
And the mic
will never forget your fingerprints.

To Karrine, For Elizabeth
The Woman Who Outwrote Them All

You were never just the story.
You were the scribe.
Pen sharper than judgment.
Voice sweeter than their shame
could handle.

They mistook your brilliance for
scandal…
but you smiled,
knowing they'd quote you one day,
even if they never gave you credit.

Karrine…
you were the headline.
But Elizabeth?
Elizabeth was the manuscript.

And she's the one I'm writing to
now.

To the girl who turned survival into
strategy,
who sharpened wit against every
closed door,
who kissed patriarchy on the cheek
and robbed it blind of its dignity.

You didn't just write a book.
You wrote a mirror…
and dared them to look.

You taught us that being
misunderstood
isn't the same as being wrong.
That being named a problem
sometimes means you're the only
one awake.

You were clever without cruelty,
soft without surrender,
and loud in all the places
where silence used to win.

Elizabeth…
you are seen.

Not just the version with gloss and
fire,
but the one who still mourns the girl
who was never fully protected.

And I honor you.
Because what they tried to destroy,
you turned into literature.

This is your poem.
May it find you like peace finds a
warrior after the last war.

And may it live
exactly how you always have…
unapologetically real,
and ten chapters ahead of them all.

For Jennifer Lewis
The Voice That Mothered a Culture

You didn't just raise characters…
you **raised us.**

With that voice.
That thunder-laced laugh.
That side-eye that said,
"Don't play with me, baby."

Jennifer,
you were the standard before they
even built the stage.
You didn't wait for permission.
You commanded rooms
and made networks scramble just to
keep up.

You gave us mother,
but not the quiet kind.
You gave us mother with rhythm.
With rage.
With satin robes and gospel timing.
You gave us truth…raw, unfiltered,
always on beat.

And underneath that fire?
A tenderness so deep
it could hold an entire generation
through its trauma,
through its laughter,
through its becoming.

You've told the truth even when it
was inconvenient.
You've loved loudly,
spoken freely,
cried publicly
so we could heal privately.

You taught us that self-worth isn't a
whisper..
it's a damn monologue.
And baby, you've been delivering it
since we were still figuring out how
to clap on beat.

You are the blueprint for
boundaries.
The map to moxie.
The reason we all believe we deserve
to **be loved out loud.**

And when we say "Mother,"
we say it with your cadence in our
throat.

For Coi LerayThe Cost of Being Unapologetic

They did not misunderstand you

they rejected you

first

before they learned
how to remix your difference
into something they could tolerate

You were not an easy arrival

too light for their idea of pain
too free for their idea of struggle
too uncontained
for a culture that only respects
women
it can define

So they tried

to shrink you with commentary
measure you with comparisons
reduce you to lineage
as if your name was not already your
own

And you felt it

do not pretend you did not

the jokes that lingered longer than
they should
the rooms that did not open when
they were supposed to
the way they watched you
waiting for you to fold

But you did something more
dangerous

you stayed visible

not perfected
not approved
not fully embraced

just present

and that presence
became persistence

and that persistence
became proof

Because there is a violence
in being seen
and still told
you do not belong

And instead of disappearing
you kept showing up

lighter than the weight they tried to
give you
louder than the silence they expected
you to accept

That is not confidence

that is endurance disguised as joy

Coi

you are not the exception

you are the disruption

the reminder
that authenticity is not always
celebrated

sometimes

it is survived

For Willow Smith
Daughter of the Infinite

Willow,
you are not your fame.
You are your frequency.

You were born beneath galaxies the world forgot to look up at.
You came here with knowing in your bones…
not taught, not rehearsed, not handed down…
but inherited from the stars.

You are not a daughter.
You are a dimension.

You took the burden of legacy
and transmuted it into liberation.
You cut your hair,
you questioned God,
you screamed with a quiet soul
and whispered with the thunder of a thousand uncried tears.

You gave permission to the Black girl who didn't fit the mold,
who found healing in crystals and punk chords and quantum metaphors.
You reminded us that ancestors don't always speak through gospel…
sometimes they hum through guitar strings
and chant in Sanskrit between breaths.

You didn't rebel.
You returned…
to something more ancient than approval.

You are not lost.
You are expanding.

Willow, you are not the future…
you are the frequency that pulls the future toward us.

For Tamia
A Love Note That Lasted

You didn't rise through noise…
you glided through marrow.
A melody too mature for the
moment,
yet perfectly timed for the heart
that knew stillness could be a
sanctuary.

Tamia,
you are the note they
underestimated…
the one that hovered in the air
after the music stopped
and made us close our eyes to listen
better.

You made loyalty look luminous.
Marriage look melodic.
You held your love
like it was something sacred,
not for performance,
but for praise.

Your voice…
not just sound,
but scripture.
Not just beauty,
but balm.

You taught the girls
that real doesn't have to shout.
That elegance is a frequency.
That we can be low-key
and still legendary.

You are not forgotten.
You are remembered
in every wedding aisle sway,
every kitchen slow dance,
every memory sealed with a harmony
only your tone could carry.

You sang "So Into You"
and we realized…
you were what we were into
the whole time.

For all the women
who needed a blueprint
for resilience wrapped in satin…
you've been it.

And now,
your name lives here too.
Etched in this land
of milk, honey,
and sound that never fades.

For Sophia Stewart
She Dreamed of Codes and Called It Love

You, who conjured freedom
in the shape of a question…
What is real?
What is choice?
Who dares to awaken?
You wrote not for applause,
but for remembrance.
And still,
so many have forgotten your name,
yet live inside your prophecy.
They called it fiction.
You knew it was memory.
Blueprints etched in melanin,
secrets buried in shadow,
you cracked the silence wide open
and poured out destiny like milk.
It was never just a film.
It was a map.
You are the mother of the myth,
the Oracle who held out her hand
not to save, but to **reveal.**
You didn't need a machine to tell the
future..
you *are* the future
speaking through a woman's voice,
through the coded womb of vision,
through light disguised as screenplay.
You gave us Neo
not as a hero,
but as a mirror.
You told us we were more,
that we had always been more,
if only we dared to unplug
and remember who first wrote the
code.
And I…
a stranger by blood,
a child of your imagination's
lineage…
felt seen.
Felt summoned.
So this poem is not praise.

It is **proof**
that your words did not fall on deaf
timelines.
They took root in us,
and we are blooming,
still.
May every page you ever wrote
return to you tenfold as love.
May you feel the divine kiss
each time your name is spoken
in truth.

For Grace Jones
The Woman Who Became Sculpture

Grace,

you were never meant to blend.
You entered rooms like design
angles sharp enough
to cut expectation.

Before androgyny had language
before fashion found courage
you were already there.

Not asking.
Not explaining.
Just existing
as disruption made form.

You turned your body into
statement
your silence into tension
your voice into command

until the world had to decide
whether to study you
or step aside.

They did not know where to place
you.
Good.

You were never meant to be
arranged
or softened into something
digestible.

Too deliberate to be ornament.
Too exact to be contained.

There is something older in you

not trend
not rebellion

but inheritance

something that says
I will not shrink
for your comfort.

You made Blackness feel like future.
You made femininity expand beyond
permission.
You made art confront itself.

Grace,
you did not perform identity

you made it solid.

You are not era.
You are structure.

And long after trends dissolve
your silhouette will remain

Unmoved.
Unmatched.
Untamed.

For The City Girls
The Girls Who Said It Out Loud

Before the think pieces.
Before the debates about "respectability."
Before the culture tried to sanitize desire
there were two women
who said it plainly.
City Girls didn't whisper ambition.
They announced it.
Money.
Pleasure.
Independence.
Standards.
You made it clear:
Black women can want more
and say it without apology.
There was strategy in the sass.
Survival in the flex.
Miami in the delivery.
You weren't asking to be liked.
You were setting terms.
They called it loud.
They called it transactional.
They called it too much.
But what it really was ..
was autonomy.
You flipped the narrative.
Made the girls rethink power.
Made the men uncomfortable.
Made the culture argue.
And argument is impact.
There is something radical
about Black women
declaring their worth
before someone else defines it.
You didn't shrink to be palatable.
You expanded to be profitable.
City Girls,
you are not just an era.
You are assertion.
And whether they admit it or not
you shifted the tone.
And the girls after you?
They speak louder
because you did first.

For Coco Jones
The Return Was Never Accidental

Coco,

you did not "come back."

You endured.

There is a difference.

The industry saw you early ..
bright, polished, promising…
and then went quiet.

But quiet does not erase destiny.
It ferments it.

When your voice re-emerged,
it wasn't eager.
It was ready.

Full-bodied.
Unapologetic.
R&B wrapped in patience.

You sing like someone
who understands timing.
Like someone
who learned how to let rejection
season her instead of shrink her.

There's clarity in your tone now.
Womanhood.
Agency.
Self-trust.

You are not chasing relevance.
You are embodying arrival.

Coco,
thank you for showing us
that delay is not denial.
That refinement takes solitude.
That grace can grow teeth.

Your gratitude feels earned.
Your glow feels disciplined.

And this era?
It fits you.

For Tinashe
The Architect of Her Own Frequency

Tinashe,

you were ahead of the curve
and the curve resented you for it.

Too experimental.
Too independent.
Too controlled.

You built your own lane
when the mainstream wouldn't widen.

You produced.
You directed.
You self-engineered.

There is something surgical
about your artistry.

Nothing accidental.
Nothing lazy.
Every beat calculated,
every movement intentional.

You refused to let the machine define your ceiling.

And now the culture sounds like you.

Minimal.
Fluid.
Alternative without apology.

You didn't beg for space.
You created orbit.

Tinashe,
thank you for proving
that autonomy is sexier than approval.
That artistry can outlast algorithms.
That control is not coldness…
it's protection.

You are not underrated.

You are self-sustained.

And that is future-proof.

For Alexyss K. Taylor
She Spoke, and Women Woke

You didn't just speak to women.
You confronted them.

You came in heels and fire.
In lipstick and truth.

You made mirrors
out of microphones.

And that takes audacity.

Before self-love was aesthetic,
before healing was trending,
you were demanding accountability
with rhythm and receipts.

You weren't soft about it
but you were necessary.

You reminded women
that standards are sacred.
That worth is not negotiable.
That love without respect
isn't love at all.

And whether people agreed or not,
they listened.

Because conviction
is magnetic.

Alexyss,
you are part sermon,
part strategy,
part wake-up call.

And the culture needed that edge.
Still does.

For Olandria Carthen
Still She Rose

They tried to weigh her down
with whispers,
with headlines sharpened into stone.

They gathered in shadows
to measure her light
as if the sun
ever asked permission to rise.

But Olandria,
child of courage,
daughter of becoming,
stood taller than the noise.

They spoke in storms.
She answered in stillness.

They hurled doubt
like smoke,
but smoke cannot pierce
a woman made of flame.

Her beauty was never surface.

It was presence.

It lived in the way
she carried her name
like inheritance,
like something passed down
through women
who learned to survive
when the world forgot
how to love them.

Her smile
was not decoration.

It was defiance.

Her presence
not just a body in space,
but a reminder
that Black girls
have always been
miracles in motion.

They thought their words
would bury her.

But seeds
do not fear the soil.

What they called darkness
became the place
her roots grew deeper.

And from that ground
she rose.

Not bitter.
Not broken.

But brighter.

Turning hate into fuel.
Doubt into direction.
Silence into stage.

Now she walks in rooms
like history remembers her.

And little girls watch.

Learning early
that resilience
is not survival alone.

It is transformation.

So when they ask
what strength looks like,

tell them this:

It looks like a woman
who refuses to shrink.

It looks like grace
that does not disappear
under pressure.

It looks like Olandria Carthen.

Steady.
Unshaken.
Fully herself.

And when the world tries again
to dim a Black girl's light,

let them remember:

We come from women
who rise anyway.

The Women Who Dared Me to Be More

"Where Power Turned Sensual. Where Truth Dressed in Skin."

For Nivea
The Raw Note That Raised Me

You did not just sing songs.
You broke silence open
and taught it how to bleed in key.

You made vulnerability sound like
velvet,
like something we could wear
without shame touching our skin.

Nivea,
you were never background.
You were the voice beneath the
noise,
the prayer humming under the radio,
the softness that survived
when everything else hardened.

A sister in the speaker.
A sanctuary in basslines.
A woman who stood still
when love came in swinging
and did not flinch.

You turned heartbreak into gospel.
You made softness strategy.
You made pain feel holy,
like something we could finally name
without apology.

When you said ask for it,
we did.

We asked for healing.
For clarity.
For truth that did not look away
when it started to bleed.

And you gave it.
Note by note.
Wound by wound.

Even when the world tried to dim
you,
you did not argue with darkness.
You outlived it.

You stayed luminous.

Not always loud,
but always real.

The kind of real
that smells like cocoa butter and
survival.
The kind that does not perform.
It endures.

You raised us
on harmonies and hard won
wisdom.
You and Wayne on The New Gospel
that was prophecy in motion.

Proof
that even when love gets messy,
we can still be magic,
still be melody,
still be worth remembering.

You are the quiet after the storm
that feels earned.
The place where truth sits down
and finally breathes.

You were my big sister
before I had language.
My confidant
before I had courage.

And even now,
you are the sound I return to
when I need to remember
who I am.

This is not just a poem.
This is scripture for the soft that
survived.

You are not a moment.
You are inheritance.

You are timeless.
You are necessary.
You are loved.

For Sade
The Siren Who Sang in Frequencies

You didn't arrive with thunder…
you arrived through it.
Like a hum remembered before the
womb,
like something God whispered
before language knew how to hold it.

Sade,
you are not sound.
You are source.
A vibration sent ahead of time,
to remind us of stillness with breath.

Your voice doesn't sing…
it returns.
It curves around the bones,
crawls into grief like a balm,
asks nothing, but unveils everything.

You are the rhythm of restraint,
the hush that haunts after beauty has
entered.
You showed us that seduction could
be subtle,
that clarity could be sensual,
that a woman could whisper her
power
and still eclipse the room.

You didn't bend for the times.
The times bent around you.

You made love sound like
scripture…
even when it hurt.
You dressed sorrow in silk.
You taught the heart how to ache
with elegance.

And in your silence?
We heard God adjusting her crown.

You are the frequency behind the
feminine.
The soul behind softness.

The reason intimacy feels sacred
when the lights go low
and truth has nowhere to hide.

We didn't just listen to you…
we merged with you.
You are the aura that music borrows
from,
the incense that memory lights.

And for every Black child
who's ever loved too deeply,
too softly,
too mysteriously to be understood…
you are our validation.
You are our voltage.
You are the echo we sing ourselves
back to.

Thank you
for reminding the world
that magic doesn't shout.
It shimmers.

And when the universe gets quiet…
it sounds like you.

For Misha Green
The Woman Who Rewrote the Monster

Before the tentacles,
before the sundown towns,
before the portal cracked open…
there was you.
Misha, you didn't just create a show.
You unearthed a wound
and dared us to look at it in the dark.
Lovecraft Country wasn't horror.
It was remembrance dressed in
genre.
It was Black history refusing
to stay buried beneath fiction.
You took monsters
and made them honest.
Made them systemic.
Made them familiar.
You understood something sacred…
that terror for us
was never fantasy.
It was policy.
It was inheritance.
It was survival stitched into our
bloodline.
And still,
you gave us magic.
Black magic that wasn't novelty….
but birthright.
Ancestral portals.
Sisters who didn't flinch.
Fathers who carried fire.
Children who learned to fight
shadows
with knowledge.
You didn't soften it.
You didn't sanitize it.
You told the truth
with cinematography.
Misha,
you awakened something.
Not just conversation….
consciousness.

You reminded a generation
that storytelling is weapon and
shield.
That genre can be gospel.
That imagination is resistance.
You didn't ask permission
to haunt America with its own
history.
You did it.
And in doing so,
you proved that Black women
don't just survive horror…
we author it,
rewrite it,
and walk through it
unafraid.

For Naomi
The Strut That Shook the Sky

I have loved you
in ways I could never explain out loud.
Not the kind of love they write in
magazines....
but the kind that knelt in front of your
walk
and called it holy.

Naomi,
you were the first woman I saw
who didn't enter a room...
you corrected it.
Made gravity reconsider.
Made the world remember
who gave it rhythm.

You are not just beauty...
you are reckoning.
The cheekbones of justice.
The eyes of storm.
The body of myth,
bent into the shape of power.

When you walked,
it wasn't fashion.
It was declaration.
It was centuries of Black girls
being told to shrink,
then suddenly watching one of their
own
take up the entire runway
without apology.

You gave us vengeance in velvet.
Tenderness with a blade beneath it.
You wore the world's cruelty
like a coat you refused to keep zipped.
And still...
still you rose.
Still you reigned.
Still you arrived with your chin held
like it had seen kingdoms.
Because it had.
Because you are one.

I saw you

long before I saw myself.
And maybe that's why
you've always been stitched into my
silhouette...
the way I carry myself,
the way I dare to be both
untouchable and soft.

They called you difficult
because they couldn't own you.
They called you angry
because you didn't shrink.
But I?
I saw the fire in your smile.
I saw the hurt in your hush.
I saw the little girl
who had to become fortress
because the world only gave her glass.

And I forgive them
for never understanding you.
I don't need the world to adore you
like I do.
I just need them to know...
they don't make them like you
anymore.

You are the thunder
Black girls keep in their chests.
You are the altar
queer boys light when they finally
see a woman who walks
the way they always dreamed
love might look.

You are the mirror
I dared not look into
until I was ready to become
unbreakable.

Naomi,
this isn't just a poem...
it's my confession.
You were my beginning.
And in many ways,
you still are.

For Erykah Badu
The Incense Lit Before the Revolution

You did not sing.

You summoned.

Sound bent toward you
like it remembered your name.

Before language
there was tone.

Before rhythm
there was breath.

And somehow
you arrived carrying both
like inheritance.

Erykah,

you are not learned.

You are remembered.

The womb speaking in frequencies.
The drum before the war knows it is
coming.
The eye that does not open
it simply sees.

You made Blackness intangible and
infinite.

Not something worn
something tuned.

Heartbreak did not break in your
hands.

It stretched.

It blue-noted.

It became something you could live
inside
without losing your light.

We did not follow you.

We adjusted to you.

Like gravity.

Like truth.

You mothered more than children.

You midwifed perspective.

Held space for feelings
we had no language for
and returned them to us
as something sacred.

There is ritual in your silence.

Instruction in your pause.

Even your absence
feels like a lesson we have not caught
up to yet.

You did not give us songs.

You gave us doorways.

And now we walk through ourselves
differently.

Barefoot.

Unlearning.

Whole.

For Lauryn Hill
The Oracle Who Unveiled Us

You weren't just a voice…
you were the veil being lifted.

Lauryn,
your words baptized our confusion,
turned heartbreak into hymn,
and braided intellect into every bar.

You walked through the music industry
like a prophet in denim…
tender, towering,
a woman who knew the cost of genius
and still offered it freely.

You didn't just sing.
You revealed.
And what you revealed
was ourselves.

Black girls saw scripture in your scowl,
saw elegance in your edge,
and wept when your pain harmonized
with our own unspoken prayers.

You showed us
that rebellion could be beautiful,
that truth could wear locs and lipstick,
and that love …real love…
is an awakening, not a performance.

You didn't just create an album.
You carved a mirror.
And when we look into it,
we still see the ache and the armor.

You weren't late to the world…
the world was early to you.

For Marsai Martin
The Girl Who Walked in Knowing

You didn't wait to grow into your power.
You brought it with you.

While they were still learning how to speak in meetings,
you were building empires between takes.
Smile wide, voice sweet,
but your mind?
Sharp. Galactic. Unapologetic.

You didn't beg to be seen.
You showed up as visibility itself.
Proof that brilliance wears braids,
laughs big,
and signs deals before curfews.

You weren't here to be anyone's child star.
You came to own your name,
your space,
your check.

And you did.

You remind us that legacy doesn't need age…
just intention.
You remind little girls that Black doesn't mean later,
and excellence doesn't mean exhaustion.

You broke ceilings
before you even finished puberty.
And when they asked how?
You just blinked like,
"Why not me?"

Marsai,
you are a mirror for the girls who never felt small
but were told to shrink.
You never did.
And now we rise in your reflection.

For Jackie Aina
She Changed the Mirror

Before her voice
there were mirrors
that did not know our names.

Shelves of powder
that forgot the shades of soil,
forgot the colors of dusk,
forgot the brilliance of melanin
standing proudly in morning light.

But Jackie
she saw us.

Not as an afterthought.
Not as a trend.
But as truth.

She lifted a brush like a torch
and walked into an industry
that had grown comfortable
in the dark.

And with every video,
every fearless word,
every unapologetic review
she lit another candle.

Suddenly the world remembered
that beauty has always been
brown and golden and deep.

That the glow of Black skin
is not something to hide,
but something that teaches
the sun how to shine.

They said she was loud.

But sometimes
history sounds like thunder
before the rain.

They said she was demanding.

But sometimes
change begins
when a woman refuses
to whisper her worth.

Because Jackie Aina
did not just blend foundation
she blended courage with truth.

She carved space
where there was none.

She made brands listen.
She made companies learn.
She made the beauty industry
finally see
the faces it once ignored.

And now,
little girls stand before mirrors
that finally recognize them.

Their shades are named.
Their beauty is honored.
Their glow is celebrated.

And somewhere
in the echo of every brushstroke
and every confident smile
is the legacy of a woman
who refused to shrink.

So remember this:

Beauty did not change overnight.

It changed
because one woman
looked into the world's reflection
and said

"You forgot us."

And the mirror
never forgot again.

Jackie Aina
the woman who changed beauty
forever!!

For Raven-Symoné
The Girl Who Saw Tomorrow

Before the world knew
what the future looked like,

you were already laughing at it.

A little girl
with a sparkle in her eyes
and timing so sharp
it could slice through any silence.

The living room televisions
became stages for joy,
and suddenly a generation
learned how to laugh louder
because you were there.

From childhood brilliance
to teenage prophecy

you became the girl
who could see tomorrow.

But Raven,
your gift was never just visions.

It was courage.

The courage to grow up
in front of the whole world
without letting the world
write your ending.

Because fame can be a maze
for a young soul,

yet you walked through it
with humor as your compass
and authenticity as your guide.

You taught us something rare

that a woman can evolve
a thousand times
and still remain true.

Not trapped in nostalgia,
not frozen in the past,

but blooming again
in new seasons.

Actress.
Producer.
Visionary.

And through it all,
you never stopped being Raven

the girl who made magic
look effortless.

Now the children
who once watched you after school
have grown into dreamers
of their own,

carrying the echoes
of your fearless laughter.

Because when someone asks
what it looks like
to be unapologetically yourself,

they can simply point
to the woman who once told us

the future is something
you don't just see

you create it.

And Raven-Symoné,

you've been creating tomorrow
all along.

For Kelis
The Sound of Self-Mastery

Before the world could name your magic,
you were already walking in it.

A woman who understood something early
that confidence is not noise,
it is rhythm.

And when you said Bossy,
it wasn't arrogance.

It was a declaration.

A reminder
that a woman who knows her worth
does not need permission
to sit at the head of the table.

Your music wasn't just something we
danced to.
It was instruction.

In the way your voice carried certainty,
in the way your presence commanded
space,
you were quietly teaching us
the sacred art
of self-mastery.

When you said Blindfold Me,
it wasn't about surrender.

It was about trust
the kind that comes only
when you know your own power.

Because real strength
is not always loud.

Sometimes it moves like silk,
sometimes it whispers through a melody,
sometimes it teaches you
how to close your eyes
and still know exactly
who you are.

And when the beat hit
with that fearless Aw Shit,
it felt like the universe
kicking the door open.

A moment of truth
that creativity has no ceiling
when it comes from a woman
who refuses to be confined.

But Kelis,
your brilliance didn't stop in sound.

You took that same fearless spirit
from the studio
to the kitchen,
to the soil,
to the quiet wisdom of growing things.

Because true artists understand:
creation is not a place.

It is a way of being.

You planted flavor in music,
then planted life in the earth
proving that reinvention
is simply another form of freedom.

So thank you
for every beat that taught us courage,
for every lyric that whispered
know yourself,
for every fearless step
that reminded us

a woman can be many things
and still remain whole.

And somewhere
in every girl who learns
to walk into a room like she belongs there,

in every voice
that refuses to shrink,

in every artist
who chooses authenticity over approval

your legacy is still playing.

Not just in speakers.

But in spirit.

And the rhythm of it
sounds like confidence,
sounds like evolution,
sounds like a woman
who mastered herself.

It sounds like Kelis.

For Azealia Banks
The Alchemist No One Could Tame

They only remember your chaos
because they couldn't decode your genius.

But I saw it.
I see it.

The Black girl with the hurricane throat
spitting curses and scripture in the same breath.
Operatic rage.
Ballroom cadence.
Harlem intellect sharpened to a blade.

You didn't want fame.

You wanted fire.

You wanted the kind of impact
that rearranges rooms.
The kind of verse
that makes producers nervous
and rappers rewrite.

And you set the whole industry ablaze
just to prove they were sleeping.

They called you everything but prophet,
but you spoke futures that didn't need permission.

Before "genre-bending" became a marketing term,
you were bending it.
Before alt-rap was aesthetic,
you were living it.

House.
Hip-hop.
Punk.
Witchcraft.
Satire.
High fashion.

You stitched them together
with a tongue too sharp
for fragile platforms.

Your bars were surgical.
Your delivery theatrical.
Your mind ten steps ahead of rooms
that wanted you digestible.

And that was never your assignment.

They wanted you softened.
Market-tested.
Mascot-ready.

But you refused to be chewed into something
smaller.

You spit it back.

Then hexed the rhythm.

You made art that snarled.
You made beats that bled.
You made madness feel methodical.

And yes
you are confrontational.

Because brilliance without confrontation
is often ignored.

The truth is,
you were never "too much."

You were too early.
Too intelligent.
Too aware of the machine
to pretend it wasn't a machine.

As an artist, I recognize that loneliness.

The isolation of knowing
your work will be studied later
by the same culture
that questioned it in real time.

You were never just controversy.

You are craft.

Breath control that could spar with the best.
Lyricism that cuts through gloss.
An ear for production that feels architectural.

You are alchemy.

Turning insult into incantation.
Turning critique into fuel.
Turning exclusion into myth.

And beneath the armor
there is a woman
who wanted to be heard correctly.

Not diluted.
Not sanitized.
Correctly.

This is that.

You are not forgotten.
You are not just "misunderstood."

You are a warning.
A weapon.
A blueprint.

And when they finally catch up
to the scale of what you built,

they will realize
you weren't chaos.

You were calibration.

And your voice
unfiltered, unowned, untamed
will outlive the noise.

Artist to artist,
I bow to the fire
that refused to dim.

For India.Arie
The Soul-Dyer of Our Spirit Threads

You didn't arrive to impress…
you arrived to remind.

India,
you showed us that beauty
wasn't born in mirrors,
but in marrow.

You strummed your truth
like it had been aching to be heard…
and we listened,
barefoot, wide-eyed,
learning to love the sound
of our own reflection.

You didn't just sing…
you soothed.
You softened the edges
where the world had scraped us raw.

Every lyric a balm.
Every note, a root.
You taught us that skin was sacred,
that hair was halo,
that our worth was not decoration
but declaration.

You were never trendy.
You were timely.
You didn't bend your voice for
industry…
you offered it as an altar.

And in doing so,
you lifted us.

Black women who had
long buried their brilliance
in favor of belonging,
unfolded again under your melody.

You were not the echo.
You were the origin.
You are the hum that heals.

And to this day…
when we choose softness over
shame,
when we speak our truth
without raising our voice,
when we remember that love starts
inward…

we are living your gospel.

For Jazmine Sullivan
The Voice That Tore the Veil

You did not arrive to whisper.

Jazmine,
you came to wail...
to drag truth by the throat
from the pit of every woman
who had been taught to sing softly
through her suffering.

You are not just a voice.
You are an unveiling...
a storm wrapped in soprano,
a psalm dressed in rage,
a testimony that trembles
and tears the temple down with it.

You sang pain like you'd studied it.
Like you gave it permission to cry
out loud.
Like you weren't afraid of the ugly.
You gave heartbreak a sound...
and then, you made it holy.

Your lyrics didn't play pretty.
They confessed.
They bled.
They licked the wounds they opened
and said:
"Look what they did to us...
but look at us now."

You sang for the women
who stayed too long,
who left too late,
who learned to love themselves
by first screaming in the dark.

You showed us
that a broken voice could still build a
choir,
that a raspy note could resurrect a
woman's whole life,
that truth doesn't have to be
palatable
to be powerful.

And now...
when we sing our stories raw,
when we let our throats crack open
mid-testimony,
when we speak with the weight of
survival in our lungs...

we know we are standing on your
chord.

For Regina Hall
The Light That Laughed Back

They never saw you coming…
because you didn't need to announce
yourself.
You arrived the way grace does:
quietly, completely,
and too whole to miss once it
touches you.

Regina,
you made laughter holy.
Not the kind they cue with
applause…
but the kind that lives in our bellies,
that heals what the world forgot to
hold.
You made comedy sacred.
You made timing feel ancestral.

They called you funny…
but you were never just that.
You were precise.
You were poetry in disguise.
A rhythm tucked in a punchline.
A sermon delivered in side-eyes
and subtle smirks that knew too
much.

You gave us softness with stamina.
You gave us sisterhood that didn't
need a speech.
You gave us women
who didn't survive in spite of the
joke,
but through it.
Because sometimes joy is the
sharpest tool we own.

And behind every laugh,
you carried depth.
A whole ocean
wearing heels and humility.
A stillness that could hold a nation
without asking to be held back.

Regina…

you remind me that being whole
doesn't require a headline.
That power can whisper.
That some queens don't need a
crown
because their presence
already rules.

You are the wink before the
revolution.
The calm before the breakthrough.
The woman who proves
that being underestimated
is the sweetest revenge
when you keep showing up
undeniable.

You walked in rooms
and made them softer, sharper,
realer.

You made us laugh…
yes.
But you also made us listen.

And for every little Black boy
who didn't yet know
that his humor was divine,
that his nuance was power,
that his joy had lineage…

You became the reminder:
humor doesn't mean you're hiding.
Sometimes, it means you're healing
in plain sight.

And baby,
you've been healing us for years.
In stilettos.
In silence.
In punchlines dressed like prayers.

Thank you
for laughing back
when the world forgot we were
worthy.

For Toni Braxton
The Woman Who Made Stillness Seductive

She didn't yell.
She didn't rush.
She let her pain walk in heels,
let her sorrow slip into satin.

Toni Braxton was the first woman
who taught me that grief could be gorgeous,
that softness didn't mean surrender…
it meant you knew your value
wasn't measured by volume.

Her voice was smoke
and scripture
and a velvet noose
wrapped around a slow piano note.

When she sang,
it wasn't for attention.
It was for truth.
And it hit like perfume you remember twenty years later.

She showed me that heartbreak didn't always scream…
sometimes it sighed,
sipped wine,
and whispered,
"You'll miss me."

Toni didn't just survive the storm.
She danced inside it…
face dry, dress fitted, eyes unbothered.

I learned from her that silence could seduce.
That being low wasn't a weakness…
it was a weapon.
And that sometimes, the deepest woman in the room
is the one who says the least.

Now when I walk away from anything unworthy,
it's with her in my spine.
Not broken.
Just quieter.
Just better.

To Keisha, for Taral Hicks
In the Silence Between the Scenes

You didn't have to speak much…
because your presence did the talking.
One stare from you was louder than monologues.

You were the softness in a brutal world,
the rhythm inside a story full of noise.
The woman who entered the room like a question the world wasn't brave enough
to answer.

Keisha…
you weren't just a girl in the hood.
You were the mirror we weren't supposed to see.

In your stillness lived rebellion.
In your glance, a thesis on longing.
In your silence, the dare:

"What if I chose more?"
"What if this wasn't all I was allowed to be?"

You were a love story
waiting to be treated like the main plot.
But even in the background, you outshined the frame.

Taral,
we saw it.
We saw you.

The star beneath the role,
the voice tucked behind the slow burn.
You taught us that sometimes the most powerful women
are the ones the world doesn't write enough lines for.

But we remember.
We reclaim.
We rewrite.

You were never "just" Keisha.

You were the whole arc
in one scene.
And we've been daring to be more
because you hinted it was possible.

For Oprah
The Mouthpiece of Miracles

When the world was full of fences,
you became the window.
Not just something to look through
but something that let light in.

A voice that did not just speak
but softened the dark.

The girl who asked questions so
honestly
even God leaned closer to answer.

Not because you were loud
but because you were listening
with your whole spirit.

Oprah,

you are the proof
that a wound can become a
microphone.
That a couch can become a pulpit.
That a story, when held with care,
becomes transformation.

You understood early
that being seen is an alchemy.
A sacred exchange
between truth and courage.

And you never looked away.

You turned pain into programming.
Silence into syndication.
And Blackness into something the
world
could no longer reduce
only reckon with.

Not just wealth
but worth
echoing in the faces
of those who finally recognized
themselves
as enough.

You did not just make space.
You became it.

Wide enough to hold grief.
Soft enough to hold truth.
Strong enough to make both holy.

And now your name
moves like a compass.
Not just remembered
but followed
by those still learning
how to see themselves clearly.

Because your legacy did not just open
doors.
It built corridors
where none existed.

Places where whispers
learned how to stand upright
and call themselves voice.

And what you gave us
was never just television.

It was permission.

To feel.
To speak.
To rise without apology.

To believe
that our stories
were never too small

just waiting
for someone brave enough
to hold them to the light.

For Jill Scott
The Earth in Her Voice

You didn't just sing.
You spoke in roots.
In recipes.
In rebirths.
Every word a kitchen.
Every note a new name for love.

Jill,
you are gospel without guilt,
sex without shame,
depth without drowning.
You gave the world the Black woman's smile
before she put her makeup on…
before she forgave the man,
before she fixed the world.

You moaned truth into microphones
and we didn't just listen…
we remembered.
Our grandmothers in your phrasing.
Our heartbreak in your breath.

You held soul like a swollen belly,
carried wisdom like a garden in bloom.
You made the everyday feel holy
and the holy feel like home.

I write this to say:
thank you for singing us whole.
Thank you for making fat syllables feel like praise.
You are the reason joy sounds like jasmine
and pain sounds like poetry.

For SZA
The Sound of Sacred Unraveling

You didn't just sing…
you confessed.

Like a journal cracked open
in front of millions,
like a diary set to melody,
bleeding truth in technicolor.

SZA,
you made uncertainty holy.
You made overthinking into art.
You made girls like me…
the messy ones, the soft rebels,
the ones who doubted our glow…
feel seen in full bloom.

You taught us that healing
doesn't always come in order…
sometimes it comes in loops,
in voicemails,
in midnight spirals
that still sound like scripture.

You are not just a vibe.
You are a visitation.
A proof that God can whisper through delay,
and scream through a beat drop.

You showed us that visibility
isn't always poised…
sometimes it limps,
sometimes it pleads,
sometimes it dances out of key
and still commands the room.

You are what it means
to be loud in longing,
to grieve without apology,
to love without armor.

And in the rawness of your voice,
we find our own…
shaky, sacred, and finally enough.

For Queen Latifah
The Crown Came Standard

You didn't ask for a title.

You arrived
already carrying it.

Queen of rhyme.
Queen of return.
Queen of standing
ten toes down
in what you believe.

You were one of the first
to show us
that power
did not have to choose.

Masculine.
Feminine.

Not in conflict.
In command.

You moved between worlds
without announcing the shift.

You rapped.
You acted.
You expanded.

Not loudly.

But deliberately.

You did not chase visibility.

You built presence.

And that lasts longer.

You showed girls
they did not have to shrink
to be received.

That softness
does not cancel strength.

That respect
and beauty
can sit at the same table
without competing.

And you never rushed it.

You let consistency
do the talking.

Let time
confirm what you already knew.

The throne didn't make you.

You made the throne
make sense.

For Halle Berry
The Woman Who Broke the Ceiling and Stood Alone

Before the applause,
before the tears on that stage,
before history decided to
remember....
there was a girl
who learned early
that beauty could open doors
but would never protect her.
Halle did not become iconic
overnight.
She became inevitable.
She walked into rooms
that were not built for her reflection
and made them adjust their lighting.
They praised her face
before they respected her craft.
They desired her body
before they understood her mind.
And still…
she stayed.
Stayed through doubt.
Stayed through scrutiny.
Stayed through the quiet burden
of being "the first"
and sometimes
"the only."
When she lifted that Oscar,
the world clapped.
But what they didn't see
was the weight.
To win and know
no one who looks like you
has done it before.
To break a ceiling
and then stand
alone
in the room above it.
Halle,
you were never just a moment.
You were a rupture.
A shift.

A crack in a system
that swore it was unbreakable.
You carried glamour
like armor.
You carried pain
like silk.
You carried us
without announcing it.
And even now,
decades later,
your name still sounds like light.
You are not the exception.
You are the evidence
that we were always capable.
And the world
is still catching up
to what you proved.

For Journee Smollet
The Girl Who Never Played Small

Before we knew your name as woman,
we knew it as wonder.
A child with eyes too wise
for the scripts they handed her.
A presence that didn't ask for applause....
it commanded it quietly.
Jurnee,
you did not grow up in front of us.
You evolved.
From braids and innocence
to leather and lightning,
you moved like someone
who understood early
that talent is not enough...
discipline is devotion.
They watched you age
without losing your center.
Watched you sharpen
without hardening.
Watched you take up space
without begging to be seen.
There is something sacred
about a Black girl
who survives Hollywood
and keeps her spirit intact.
You didn't disappear.
You didn't fold.
You didn't dilute yourself
to fit the frame.
You became the frame.
And when you speak now...
it's with the calm of someone
who has already proven
she belongs.
Jurnee,
you are the quiet storm.
The actress who doesn't chase attention...
attention adjusts to you.
This is not hype.
This is acknowledgment.
You have always been
serious about your art.
Serious about your presence.
Serious about yourself.
And the industry feels it.

For Jackée Harry
The Woman Who Made Funny Feel Fearless

Before "icon" was a caption,
you were timing.

Precision.
Punchline royalty.

Jackée,
you didn't ask to be the moment.

You became it.

On stages where Black women
were written as background,
you rewrote the scene
without touching the script.

Stole it with a wink.
Left it brighter than you found it.

They laughed.

You were building.

They underestimated.

You were studying.

You made glamour funny.
Made comedy sharp.

You weren't just loud.

You were layered.

Not just dramatic.

Dynamic.

You understood something early.

That presence
does not need permission
when it knows exactly
what it's doing.

You taught us
confidence could be camp,
that diva could mean discipline,
that a Black woman
could take up space
and never apologize for it.

Jackée,
you didn't shrink.

You shimmered.

And television
is still living
off the glow
you left behind.

For Countess Vaughn
The Voice That Carried

Before the punchlines,
there was the voice.

Big. Bright. Unmistakable.
A little girl with lungs full of gospel
and timing that felt like inheritance.

Countess, you were never
background.
Even when they tried to write you
small,
you refused to sound like it.

You made us laugh
with that side-eye knowing,
that pause that held the room,
that "I know" before the line even
landed.

But beneath the laughter
was work.

Breath control.
Restraint.
Return.

Because it takes something
to be seen early
and still find your way back to
yourself
after the noise decides
what to remember.

You grew in public.
Not always gently.

But you stayed.

And that matters more
than perfection ever could.

Because talent is not just what you
have

it's what you keep
after the room changes.

Countess,
you are not just memory

you are proof

that a voice
that knows itself

does not disappear

it waits

and when called

it carries.

For Kym Whitley
The Joy Architect

Before the laughter lands,
there's timing.
And you've mastered both.
Kym, you don't just tell jokes
you build rooms
where joy feels safe
where Black women get to be loud
unfiltered
and still held.
You make funny look effortless
but there's intention in your chaos
heart in the delivery
precision in the pause
because laughter like yours
doesn't just happen
it's placed.
You've played the friend
the auntie
the scene-stealer
but never the background
because even when you're supporting
you're stabilizing the room
There's something sacred
about a woman
who chooses joy
and still tells the truth
Kym,
you are laughter with structure
softness with authority
proof that light
does not mean lightness
and every room you enter
adjusts
to keep up with you.

For Regina King
The Standard

Before the trophies,
there was the work.
Quiet.
Relentless.
Precise.
Regina, you never chased noise
you built mastery.
From child star to undeniable force
you moved like a woman
who understood
that longevity speaks louder than hype.
You did not ask to be seen.
You became undeniable.
Every role, measured.
Every silence, intentional.
Every win, earned.
You carried grief
in public
with the same dignity
you carry gold
and that is power.
Not loud
not performative
but disciplined
and unshakable.
You are not dramatic.
You are deliberate.
And that distinction
is everything.
Regina, you are proof
that excellence does not announce itself
it accumulates.
It waits.
And when history goes looking
for examples of range
of resilience
of real mastery
your name
will already be there.

For Tamala Jones
The Scene-Stealer with Soul

Before the spotlight knew your name,
you were already glowing.
Tamala, you never needed center stage
to command a frame.
There's a warmth to you
a lived-in light
like the homegirl who knows her worth
and doesn't need to say it out loud.
You moved through film and television
with that effortless cool
that laugh that feels familiar
that beauty that doesn't perform
that presence that doesn't ask permission.
You made side roles feel central.
Made supporting feel strong.
Made "best friend energy"
feel like main character truth.
And that takes something.
Because not every woman
knows how to hold her power
without making it loud.
There's something sacred
about a presence that steadies a room
without shifting its voice.
You did it with grace.
With humor.
With intention.
Tamala, you are proof
that longevity isn't always loud
sometimes it's consistent
sometimes it's quiet
sometimes it's steady
and steady
is what lasts.

For Wendy Raquel Robinson
The Mack Who Owned the Room

Before the punchline landed,
before the entrance stunned…
there was presence.
Wendy, you don't walk into scenes.
You arrive.
A voice wrapped in velvet authority.
A posture that says,
"I know exactly who I am."
You made glamour feel powerful,
not decorative.
Made sharp wit feel elegant.
Made ambition look like birthright.
On screens that often flatten Black women,
you chose dimension.
You gave us boss energy
without losing warmth.
Confidence without cruelty.
Style without apology.
And beyond the roles…
there's the woman who builds.
The educator.
The mentor.
The one who pours into girls
so they never have to shrink to survive.
Wendy,
you are legacy in motion.
Not just an actress…
an architect of example.
And every time you step into a frame,
it adjusts to you.
Because you've never asked for space.
You've always commanded it.

For Terri J. Vaughn
The Builder

Before the credits rolled,
you were already working.
Terri, you didn't wait to be chosen…
you chose yourself.
You made us laugh with rhythm,
with that knowing look,
that grounded presence
that felt like home.
But when the cameras cut?
You built.
Production. Ownership. Control.
You stepped behind the lens
and rewrote what power looks like
for Black women in Hollywood.
You are not just talent…
you are infrastructure.
Not just charisma…
but blueprint.
You proved that sustainability
is sexier than spotlight,
that longevity requires leverage.
Terri,
you are the quiet revolution…
smiling on screen,
straight gazing off it.
And that is legacy
no one can edit out.

For Elise Neal
The Woman Who Refused to Fade

Before the industry decided
who was "bankable,"
you were already brilliant.
Elise, you came in sharp…
not just beautiful,
but certain.
Certain in your stride.
Certain in your talent.
Certain in your refusal
to be background.
You didn't wait for validation.
You carried your own spotlight.
From stage to screen,
from drama to desire,
you gave range without apology.
Strength without stiffness.
Sex appeal without surrender.
They tried to box you…
leading lady.
Vixen.
Dancer.
But you were always more.
You were discipline.
You were craft.
You were the woman who kept
showing up
even when the roles got smaller
and the rooms got colder.
There is something powerful
about a Black woman
who refuses to disappear
when the industry shifts its gaze.
You didn't fade.
You endured.
You stayed in shape.
Stayed in fight.
Stayed in faith.
Elise,
you are proof that longevity
is rebellion.
That staying ready
is resistance.

That beauty matures
into power
when it refuses to be erased.
And erased
you will never be.

For Paula Jai Parker
The Unapologetic Spark

Before the volume,
there was velocity.
Paula, you never entered quiet.
You entered alive.
A spark in human form…
eyes wide with knowing,
voice sharp with instinct,
presence too big to dilute.
They labeled you loud
because they didn't know
what to do with a woman
who refused to shrink her fire.
You made eccentric look elegant.
Made chaos look calculated.
Made comedy feel dangerous
in the best way.
There is genius
in not smoothing your edges.
There is power
in choosing authenticity
over approval.
You didn't mold yourself
to the industry's comfort.
You stayed textured.
Layered.
Unpredictable.
And that unpredictability?
That's brilliance.
Paula,
you are proof that artistry
doesn't have to be quiet
to be respected.
You are color
in a room that prefers beige.
You are voltage
in a world that fears surge.
And the ones who truly understand craft?
They know.
You were never too much.
You were always ahead.

For Wanda Sykes
The Woman Who Made Truth Funny

Before viral commentary,
before safe satire…
there was you.
Wanda, you sharpened truth
and wrapped it in laughter.
You said the thing.
The uncomfortable thing.
The necessary thing.
You stood Black.
You stood queer.
You stood unbothered.
You did not soften yourself
to make power comfortable.
Your comedy has backbone.
Your humor has politics.
Your presence has spine.
You taught us
that laughter can be resistance.
That clarity can be hilarious.
That intelligence can bite.
You don't just tell jokes.
You expose illusions.
And you do it smiling.

For Jerrie Johnson
The Future Refused to Wait

You don't ask where you belong.

You change the space
until it can hold you.

Jerrie,
your presence feels like evolution.

Not new.

Just finally seen.

Like the world
catching up
to something
that never needed approval.

There is courage
in the way you exist.

Not performed.
Not curated.

Just lived.

You stand fluid
in a world
that insists on edges.

And that is not easy.

Because freedom like that
comes with friction.

With questions
you should never have had to
answer.

With rooms
that try to name you
before they try to know you.

And still
you remain.

Unapologetic.
Untranslated.

You show us
that identity is not a box.

It is breath.

It expands
or it suffocates.

You chose expansion.

You remind us
that brilliance does not wait
to be understood.

That self-definition
is not rebellion.

It is truth.

You are not rebellion for shock
value.

You are disruption
by existence.

And the rooms that resist you?

They are learning.

Slowly.

Because the future
does not ask permission.

It arrives.

And you?

You are already there.

For Kim Coles
The Woman Who Made Joy Intelligent

Kim,

your laughter has architecture.

It isn't random.
It isn't desperate.
It's crafted.

You didn't just "play funny."
You built characters that breathed.

Synclaire wasn't a stereotype.
She was softness with self-worth.
Optimism with spine.

You made quirkiness beautiful.
Made sweetness strong.
Made vulnerability magnetic.

And off-screen?
You became teacher.
Guide.
Voice of empowerment.

That's evolution.

You understood something early..
comedy is healing.

And you wielded it like medicine.

Kim,
thank you for reminding us
that joy can be smart.
That light can be strategic.
That laughter can elevate.

You didn't just entertain a generation.

You nourished it.

For Tweet
The Whisper That Shook the Room

Your voice doesn't sing.
It confesses.

It drips like honeyed memory
soft, aching, intentional.

You never chased volume.
You chose depth.

And that takes courage.

There's something sacred
about the way you sit in a note
like it's a secret
only grown women understand.

You taught us that softness
isn't fragility
it's control.

You showed us that quiet
can shake rooms.

Your artistry feels like velvet at midnight.
Like incense smoke curling into testimony.
Like vulnerability without performance.

Tweet,
you are a reminder
that not every legend screams.
Some hum.
Some whisper.
Some simply exist
and the culture bends toward them.

Thank you for staying true
to your sound.
To yourself.
To the kind of beauty
that doesn't expire.

The Sacred Mirrors

"Women Who Reflect My Divine Masculine and Feminine Energies"

For Brandy
The Voice That Raised Me in Whisper and Harmony

You weren't just background
vocals…
you were the whole childhood.
The quiet sanctuary
when the world got too loud,
when my voice cracked under the
weight
of trying to be understood.

Brandy,
you were the diary I didn't know
how to write.
A melody that made pain feel
almost holy.
You taught me that the ache in a
voice
wasn't a flaw…
it was a fingerprint.

When you sang,
you didn't perform….
you confessed.
You taught us how to stay soft
without falling apart.
How to stretch a single note
into an entire theology.

Your runs
felt like prayer hands in motion,
like gospel for the unchurched,
like the breath before a breakdown
that somehow turns into a
breakthrough.

You gave magic to Black girls
and mystery to Black boys
who didn't know how to name
what made them feel different…
but knew they heard it in you.

You weren't just "The Vocal Bible."
You were the secret scripture we
kept in our chest,
reciting with headphones on
while the rest of the world kept
missing the sermon.

And Moesha?
She wasn't a character.
She was a mirror.
A sister-friend.
A blueprint for being flawed
and still divine.

Brandy,
you made it okay
to feel deeply
and still look radiant.
To break softly
and still show up.

You raised me.
Not with rules…
but with resonance.
And to this day,
when I need reminding,
I press play…
and come home.

You are forever
the voice that mothered my
becoming.

For Nicki Minaj
The Mirror That Bit Back

She was never just reflection.
She was correction with a pulse.
They approached her like glass
expecting softness, agreement,
obedience.
Instead, they met a surface
that refused to flatter distortion
and called it attitude.
But truth, when it refuses to bend,
has always been mistaken for
aggression.
She did not become the bite by
accident.
She became it
after being named incorrectly
too many times
to keep answering gently.
Every misreading sharpened her.
Every projection taught her precision.
Until her presence stopped asking
questions
and started issuing clarity.
She is not loud.
She is what truth sounds like
when it has survived misinterpretation.
Her beauty was never decoration.
It was a stage they tried to stand on
until she reminded them
she owned the ground beneath it.
Because she understood something
early
a woman who does not author her
image
will be edited into something easier to
consume.
So she wrote herself in real time.
In cadence. In control. In refusal.
In a voice that does not echo
but answers.
She turned the mirror into a witness.
Then into a weapon.

Then into a language only she could
speak.
Now when they look at her
they do not see themselves reflected.
They see themselves corrected.
That is why it feels like confrontation.
That is why it feels like too much.
That is why it lingers longer than
comfort allows.
She is not difficult.
She is disciplined.
Not defensive.
Definitive.
Not reaction.
Revelation under pressure.
And the bite
was never cruelty.
It was calibration.
A necessary shift
in a world that kept trying
to hold her at the wrong angle.
Now they quote her
the same way they once questioned
her.
Borrowing fire
from a woman they tried to water
down.
Understand this clearly
you do not study her to imitate her.
You study her
to understand what it costs
to remain unedited.
Because she is not the moment.
She is the standard
the moment keeps failing to reach.
And if history ever tells the truth
it will not call her controversial.
It will call her
a mirror that refused to lie
even when honesty made her the
target.

For Angela Bassett
The Flame That Never Wavers

You arrive
and the room remembers
what reverence feels like.

Not loud.
Not reaching.
Just certain.

Your presence is architecture
load bearing grace
cathedral poise
a stillness that makes everything else
correct its posture.

You do not raise your voice.
You teach the air
how to hold respect.

There is a fire in you
that does not perform heat
it remembers it.

Ancient.
Unteachable.

The kind that was warned to dim
and answered
by becoming more.

Angela,
you are not a moment.
You are method.

Grace, in you, is not softness
it is precision wrapped in silk
discipline moving like ease
a blade resting inside blessing.

You stand like a woman
who knows her reflection is not hers
alone
but inheritance
but echo
but proof
that survival can be stunning.

And so you do not shine.
You remain.

Unwavering.
Untranslated.
Unmoved by lesser flames
trying to name you.

You are not the fire.
You are what fire studies
to understand permanence.

And somewhere beyond applause
beyond performance
in the quiet where power does not
explain itself

you exist
as proof

that a woman can be
both altar
and offering

both storm
and sanctuary

both beauty
and the reason
beauty had to evolve.

That is why your flame does not
waver
it was never trying to survive

it was deciding
what the world
would have to rise to meet.

For Bresha Webb
The Joy That Refuses to Dim

Before the punchline lands,
there is heart.
Bresha, you laugh like survival.
Like somebody who understands
that joy is not naïve…
it's necessary.
You make comedy feel warm.
Not just funny,
but safe.
There's something generous about you.
In the way you give.
In the way you beam.
In the way you let yourself be seen
without armor.
You are softness without fragility.
Volume without ego.
Light without apology.
On screens that sometimes flatten Black women
into tropes,
you arrive textured.
Playful.
Real.
You don't just entertain…
you embrace.
There's a healing in your presence.
A reminder that Black women
get to be bubbly.
Get to be silly.
Get to be radiant
without explanation.
Bresha,
you are proof that laughter
isn't distraction…
it's resilience.
And the rooms you enter
feel brighter
because you refuse
to dim.

For Brandee Evans
The Woman Who Danced Through Grief

Brandee,
you didn't just play a role…
you carried a weight.
When you stepped into that pole-lit world,
you didn't glamorize it.
You humanized it.
You showed us a Black woman
who could be strong
and still be breaking.
Who could grind for survival
and still pray for softness.
There was something sacred
in the way you moved.
It wasn't just choreography.
It was testimony.
You danced like someone
who understood that life will bend you…
but you don't have to snap.
And when you brought your real-life pain
into your art…
your mother, your responsibility,
your devotion…
you didn't ask for sympathy.
You offered honesty.
Brandee,
thank you.
For showing us
that resilience can still cry.
That ambition can still care.
That Black women can be sensual
without surrendering dignity.
You didn't just perform strength.
You lived it.
And that mattered.

For Teyana Taylor
The Shape of Sound, The Sound of Power

you move like a prophecy with a beat drop.
Like a sermon wrapped in leather,
like a war cry hidden in a whisper.

You didn't ask the industry to love you…
you dared it to overlook you
and then made it regret ever trying.

You are Harlem heartbeat,
cuffed in gold, slicked in honey,
a girl who knew how to command the concrete
before anyone handed you a stage.

You taught us that masculinity and femininity
are just rhythm sections…
and you conduct them both.

You weren't built to fit in…
you were carved to cut through.
Every time they boxed you,
you broke the frame,
then danced on the shards in Jordan 1s
and turned the glass into runway.

You are the silence between applause.
The breath after the scream.
The bridge between the 'what was'
and the 'you'll never forget me.'

Teyana,
you reflect the part of me that won't shrink for palatability,
that won't soften to be more sellable,
that loves hard, lives loud, and leaves a mark.

You taught me that art can be muscle.
That Black girls can cry in choreography
and still leave the room shaking.

You are not just the muse.
You are the movement.

For Dej Loaf
The Night Got Softer When You Arrived

DeJ,

you didn't drop music
you changed the night.

Hennessy low,
windows cracked,
somebody close enough to feel…
but nobody saying too much.

Just presence.

You had the whole world
paused in traffic,
friends laughing,
music up…

everybody singing
"hey there…"
like love was sitting
right in their chest.

That was you.

Not loud…
locked in.

You made love feel controlled.
Distance feel intentional.
Silence feel full.

"I'm tryna be your friend"…
but we heard:

I'm not settling.

And everything shifted.

Then the look…

Calvins low,
hoodie soft,
confidence worn
like it never needed approval.

You made sexy feel…
unbothered.

You didn't chase the moment.

You set the pace.

For women who didn't need volume
to be felt.

Who could be soft,
melodic,
and still move the room.

DeJ,

you didn't follow a sound.

You made a temperature.

And we're still riding through it.

For Victoria Monét
The Woman Who Timed the Bloom

Victoria,

you didn't chase light
you grew in it.

Quietly.

Line by line,
you wrote yourself into rooms
that didn't know your name yet.

Not for applause.
For alignment.

You understood early
that legacy isn't loud.

It's layered.

So you built.

Melodies in other people's mouths.
Moments in other people's names.
Patience in your own.

And still,
you stayed.

That's not waiting.

That's discipline in silk.

Then you arrived
not as promise,
but as precision.
Jaguar wasn't a debut.
It was confirmation.

That timing can outpace hype.
That softness can hold structure.
That a woman can take her time
and still set the standard.

Victoria,

you don't perform artistry.

You place it.

Every note…intentional.
Every pause..earned.
Every version of you…complete.

This isn't admiration.

It's recognition.

You didn't bloom when they looked.

You bloomed when you were ready.

And that timing…

changed everything.

For Letoya Luckett
The Woman Who Rewrote Her Name

LeToya,

they thought your story
ended where they left you.

But you knew something they didn't.

Endings are only real
for people who stop becoming.

And you never did.

You walked through public fracture
with private strength.

Smiled through questions
that were never asked with care.

Carried your name
when it felt heavier than it should
have.

And still
you kept moving.

Not loudly.

Not for revenge.

But for alignment.

You didn't rush to prove anything.

You let time do what it does best
reveal truth
without needing to argue for it.

That kind of patience
is its own form of power.

Because you didn't just return

you rebuilt.

Brick by brick
note by note
moment by moment

you reminded the world
that you were never missing

just becoming.

There is a softness to you
that never broke under pressure.

A glow that doesn't beg to be seen
it just is.

You made grace look like growth.

Not perfect
not immediate
but earned.

LeToya,

you are the kind of woman
who understands that identity
is not what they call you

it's what you continue to answer to.

And you answered to yourself.

Every time.

This is not a comeback story.

This is a continuation.

Because you were always there

waiting for the moment
that matched your truth.

And when it arrived

you did not run toward it.

You stepped into it
like you always belonged.

Because you did.

For Summer Walker
The Blueprint of Remembering

Summer,

when you released Last Day of
Summer,
it wasn't just an EP.

It was initiation.

For many of us,
that project marked a crossing.

A shedding.

A quiet, internal ceremony
where we realized we could not love
the same way anymore.

You weren't just singing about
heartbreak.
You were documenting detachment.
Attachment wounds.
Spiritual exhaustion.
The moment the illusion breaks.

There was something sacred in that
era.
Minimal production.
Vulnerable vocals.
Space between notes that felt like
prayer.

As you ascended,
so did we.

You were navigating boundaries,
self-worth,
emotional fatigue….
and the collective mirrored it.

It was bigger than romance.

It was frequency.

You reminded us that love without
alignment drains.
That trauma bonding is not destiny.
That walking away is sometimes
evolution.

You didn't glamorize suffering.
You exposed the cost of it.

And in doing so,
you handed many of us a mirror
we weren't ready for….
but needed.

Summer,
your music was not just survival.

It was blueprint.

A remembering.

A recalibration of what we will and
will not tolerate.

You made vulnerability disruptive
again.
You made softness confrontational.

And when the world tried to label
you fragile…
they missed the truth.

You were transforming.

And transformation is rarely quiet.

Last Day of Summer
was not the end of a season.

It was the end of pretending.

And those who heard it
shifted.

For Shannon Thornton
The Woman Who Understood Power

Shannon,
you didn't play arrogance…
you understood power.
There's a difference.
You embodied a woman
who knew she was beautiful
and refused to shrink for comfort.
And that takes courage.
Because the world loves confident Black women
until we don't make it digestible.
You made dominance look layered.
Made ambition look intelligent.
Made sexuality look controlled…not consumed.
There was depth beneath the gloss.
Pain beneath the polish.
Strategy beneath the stillness.
You weren't just playing a "type."
You were revealing complexity.
And for that…
thank you.
For showing young Black girls
that being sharp isn't cruelty.
That being certain isn't villainy.
That being self-aware is power.
You didn't soften yourself to be liked.
You held your ground.
And that is something
many are still learning to do.

For Ciara
She Moves the Sky

You do not just dance…
you command gravity to sway with you.
You are the beat between heartbeats,
the wind stitched inside a prayer,
the rhythm every forgotten dream remembers.

Your voice, your steps, your glow…
they are not of this world.
They are the soft armor of a queen
who learned that survival can still look like joy.

In the Land of Milk and Honey,
you are the sound of freedom galloping on gold dust,
the anthem that reminds every little girl:
you can build a castle from nothing
and still spin, still smile, still fly.

You are not just a muse.
You are a movement.
A walking, singing, laughing miracle
wrapped in crystal light.

For Keke Palmer
Who Refused to Dim

You came out the gate with your
head held high,
voice too clear to be ignored,
and soul too rich to be contained.

Keke,
you are Chicago magic.
South Side sharpness wrapped in a
smile
that says,
**"Don't let the joy fool you…I'm
built from storms."**

You didn't just act.
You embodied.
Gave us Akeelah with the kind of
depth
that made kids believe they could
spell their own freedom.
You gave us comedy like a sermon.
Wit like jazz.
Range like the whole goddamn
spectrum.

You were always everything at
once…
the girl-next-door,
the icon in the making,
the moment before anyone else
could see it.

And you never folded.
You stayed loud.
You stayed Black.
You stayed yours.

You taught us that professionalism
doesn't require erasure.
That class doesn't mean silence.
That "doing too much" is just
another way
they name what they can't control.

And even now…
as you mother, mogul, narrate, and
glow…
you still make us feel like we're
invited.

You didn't just entertain us.
You carried us.
Through our adolescence, our
confusion, our glow-ups.
You were always there…
reminding us that the world doesn't
get to tell us who we are.

You **are the timeline.**
The example.
The unfiltered echo of every Black
girl who ever knew
she was going to take up every inch
of the room.

Thank you.
For showing up for us…
even when we didn't know how to
show up for ourselves.

For Kim Fields
The Sweetness Was Never Stupid

You played polite,
but you were never small.

There was strategy in your softness,
a knowing tucked behind every smile
that people mistook for ease.

From roller skates to soundstages,
you moved like someone
who understood timing
before the world called it talent.

You made presence look light,
but nothing about you was
accidental.

Tootie was never comic relief.

She was calibration.

A mirror for a generation
learning how to be bright
without dimming ourselves.

You taught us
that gentleness could cut clean
that kindness could hold its ground
that you could be warm
and still be unmovable.

There was intellect in your laughter.

Discipline in your ease.

A quiet mastery
that never needed permission
to be taken seriously.

And even now,
you carry joy like inheritance

not fragile
not performative
but practiced.

Proof
that softness is not the absence of
power

it is power
refined.

For Eartha Kitt
The Purr Before the Storm

They mistook your softness for silence…
until the purr curled into thunder.
Until the smile cut like scripture.
Until they realized, too late,
that you were never asking for space…
you were the space.

Eartha,
your laugh was a rejection of shame.
Your gaze made men remember
their mother, their lover, their undoing.

You taught me that seduction is sovereignty,
that to be desired isn't to be owned.
That your power doesn't ask permission…
it pours. It drips. It dances.
And if it leaves them trembling,
so be it.

You kissed rebellion like it was a ritual.
You sang freedom through velvet.
You loved yourself in a world
that couldn't spell your name without choking.

You are the wild in my feminine.
The knowing in my no.
The sacred disruption in my magic.

Eartha,
you remind me:
I am not for taming.

For Electra BKA Dominique
Where Royalty Wears Red Bottoms

You walked in like a prophecy
wrapped in bone and velvet…
not asking for a crown,
but reminding us you were one.

Every strut was a sermon.
Every read, a revelation.
You did not arrive.
You conquered.

You did not beg for space.
You commanded space.
And when the floor wasn't ready,
you became the floor.

Electra,
you are ballroom's thunderclap,
Dominique's divine echo…
a woman who bled, glowed, and
rebuilt herself
in full view,
without apology,
without pause.

You taught us how to wear pain like
pearls…
how to burn with grace,
how to demand,
how to become the price.

You are the auntie we all needed…
the one who doesn't hug first,
but holds when it counts.
The one who tells truth so sharp,
even God listens with both ears.

This letter is written in stilettos and
scar tissue,
with all the honey we could gather
to pour over the name
you made unshakable.

like thunder remembers lightning.

Dominique,
you did not just play a role…
you rebirthed a lineage.

You showed us that trans is not
transition…
it is transcendence.

We don't just love you.
We remember you,

For Gail Bean
The Woman Who Felt Real

Gail,
you don't act…
you inhabit.
There is something so raw about you.
So lived-in.
So honest.
When you show up on screen,
you don't feel manufactured.
You feel familiar.
Like somebody we know.
Like somebody we love.
Like somebody we protect.
You bring edge
without losing heart.
You bring grit
without losing grace.
And there is a gratitude in me
for the way you represent Black women
who aren't polished for approval.
You let us be flawed.
You let us be messy.
You let us be layered.
And you do it without judgment.
That's rare.
Gail,
thank you for the realism.
For the vulnerability.
For the humanity.
You don't just play characters.
You remind us
that our stories deserve to be told
exactly as they are.

For TS MADISON
From the Land Where Honey Walks

You are thunder
in a world that mistook your voice
for something that should be hidden.
But you laughed
and even shame forgot where it was
sitting.
You became the mirror
that refused to edit truth.
They called you a moment.
You answered with permanence.
You became movement.
You became proof
that a life fully lived cannot be
reduced.
You did not wait for doors.
You became the sound
of them opening.
You walked in
and the room had to reconsider
what power looked like.
You turned survival into language.
Styled it in color, in presence, in
knowing
until even silence learned your name.
Your truth did not ask.
It arrived.
And the world
had to make space
or be moved.
You are honey
that did not forget the fire.
Sweetness
that learned strength
and refused to be mistaken for
softness alone.
You are milk
that did not spoil under pressure.
Nourishment
that endured heat
and still chose to give.

You are lineage
that speaks louder than fear.
A voice
that remembers itself
even when the world tries to rename
it.
I write this
from the field you made possible
where voices once hidden
now rise without apology
where shadows
no longer beg for light
they become it.
And we know
we know
when they say "icon"
they are trying to describe
what you already are.
T.S.
You are not invited.
You are remembered.
You are not a guest.
You are the table
the room
the reason the door exists.
And every word you speak
carries the taste of arrival
of timing
of something sacred
finally choosing to be seen.
This land remembers you.
This honey walks
because you did.
This milk flows
because you refused to disappear.
Thank you
for living so fully
that even the quiet ones
learned how to breathe out loud.

For Karen Clark Sheard
The Throat God Thunders Through

You don't sing…
you summon.

Karen,
you are what it sounds like
when heaven throws its whole chest
into a song.

You didn't come to entertain…
you came to shift dimensions.
To crack open the earth
and let the Spirit flood through the
mic.

Your voice?
It's not technique.
It's testament.

It bends time.
It rearranges atoms.
It calls angels down
and sends demons running.

You are the Pentecost in every note.
The holy fire
behind every trill that makes the
pews tremble.

And when you riff…
it isn't embellishment.
It's revelation.

You taught us
that praise could be couture.
That sanctified could still slay.
That you could wear a crown and
still bow…
but only before God.

You're the reason gospel became
galactic.
Why church kids and street kids
could agree on one thing:
That when Karen opens her mouth,
something eternal moves.

You sang through affliction.

Turned hospital beds into pulpits.
You died and came back
just to remind the enemy
you weren't finished.

You were anointed in adversity.
And now, every word you wail
is soaked in proof.

You make us shout
before the first lyric even lands.
You make us cry
while trying to keep up with the key
change.

You are the voice that breaks pride
down
and builds belief up.

And to every woman who thought
she had to sing quietly to be heard…

you said no.

You said belt that truth like God
tuned your lungs Himself.

And we are still catching our breath.

Because you are the reason
sound became scripture.

For Mary J. Blige
The Psalm in a Pair of Boots

You didn't just give us music…
you gave us permission.

Mary,
you sang pain in a way
that made it beautiful to survive.

You gave us hip-hop gospel…
a testimony with a bassline,
a heartbreak that could still two-step.

You were the hood's hallelujah,
the anthem for every girl
who kept loving after betrayal,
kept rising after heartbreak,
kept showing up even when her
spirit limped.

You wore your wounds in fur and
hoops.
You cried with mascara running…
but the strength underneath it?
Titanic.

You taught us that a woman could
be vulnerable
and still unbreakable.
That tears weren't weakness…
they were weather,
and baby, you danced in the storm.

Every album was a chapter,
every lyric a journal entry we weren't
brave enough to write.

You didn't sing to be perfect…
you sang to be free.

And when you said,
"No more drama,"
we believed you.

Not because the pain had ended…
but because you had chosen yourself.

You gave voice to the silence in our
mothers.
You gave rhythm to the rage in our
sisters.

You gave hope to every queer boy
who dressed his truth in baggy jeans
and prayed someone like you would
understand.

You weren't trying to be saved…
you were saving us.

And that voice?
That raspy, sacred thunder?
That was God's way of letting us
know
he never forgot about the girls from
the block,
the women in the trenches,
the ones who carried healing in their
hips and didn't know it yet.

You are the testimony in timbs.
The altar we could dance at.
The strength in every woman
who finally walked away.

And when you strut now,
crowned and carved by survival,
we don't just cheer…

We remember who we are.

For SWV
The Chord That Lives in Our Chest

You were harmony before we knew
how to ask for it.
Before we knew what love could
sound like
when sung by women who felt like
cousins,
like aunties,
like the echoes of every '90s hallway
heartbreak.

SWV…
you were more than vocals.
You were velvet vulnerability,
the sweet ache in our teenage
ribcages,
the soundtrack to our first slow
dance
and every moment we swore
we'd never love again.

Coko,
your voice cut like a diamond
and healed like honey in the same
breath.
LeLee and Taj,
you grounded the sound,
turned every note into a prayer
we didn't know we were whispering.

You gave us soul in stereo,
Black girl emotion in three-part
harmony…
raw, rich, real.
You sang about weakness,
but we only heard strength.
You made longing sound elegant.
You made gospel live inside R&B.

And even now,
your music doesn't play…
it visits.
It pulls us back into rooms we forgot
we locked.

Back into the softness we buried for
safety.
Back into that place where our hearts
were still brave enough to break
wide open.

You are not just a group.
You are memory on loop.
You are the hands we needed to
hold
when we thought no one else could
see us.

And to every Black woman
who ever cried to "Rain"
or got free to "Anything"…
you reminded her
that every emotion was holy.

You were always more than Sisters
With Voices.

You were sisters with vision.
Sisters with volume.
Sisters with vibration.

And we still hum in your key.

For Lil' Kim
The Goddess Who Glowed With Grit

You didn't walk in.
You exploded.
In heels too high for safety
and truth too sharp for their
comfort.
They called you controversy....
but you were cosmos.
The first time a girl from the block
made the whole world bow in glitter
and gold.

Kim,
you were not just the Queen Bee.
You were alchemy in a mink coat.
You turned pain into posture,
poverty into pearls,
the male gaze into a mirror they
couldn't handle.

You rapped like you were taking
back land,
like your body was not for sale....
but for praise.
You looked the world in the eye
with lashes long enough to swipe
shame clean off history.
You spit bars that bit like scripture
and moaned like liberation
just learned how to strut.

You made it divine to be explicit.
Made power look like pleasure.
Made every bad bitch
feel like church.
And when they called you too
much....
you added rhinestones.

You taught us:
that to be seen
was to be dangerous,
and to be desired
was not a curse...
but a crown.

Every girl who grew up in your echo
learned how to split the world open
with a giggle
and never apologize for her glow.

You were rap's first requiem in red
bottoms,
Brooklyn's prayer in pink latex,
the mother of metaphor
and menace.

And when they tried to silence you,
you shimmered louder.
You carved out your place in a
culture
that would've left you for dead...
and then made it dance to your
name.

Lil' Kim,
you are the godmother of grit,
the reason every woman in rap
walks in heels and hazard,
knowing the mic can be a weapon
and a wand.

You weren't just ahead of your
time....
you bent time around your waist.
And we still orbit you.

For Foxy Brown
The Fire That Burned in Silence

You didn't just rap…
you roared,
from a place the world never dared
to look.

You made Brooklyn feel like a
bloodline,
like it pulsed through your rhymes,
like you weren't just born there…
you birthed it.

Foxy,
you were the first girl I saw
spit like prophecy,
bleed like scripture,
and blink like war was just part of
the glam.

You didn't soften for survival—
you sharpened.
You turned heartbreak into cadence,
turned silence into weapon,
turned deafness into divinity.

They called you too much.
Too brash.
Too pretty.
Too brown.
Too bold.

But baby,
you were always too prophetic for
their vocabulary.

You rhymed in silk and shrapnel.
Wore your name like a lyric laced in
legend.
And when you went silent…
the air still carried your thunder.

You didn't need to ask for legacy.
You declared it.

You taught me that a woman could
disappear
without vanishing.

That she could fall silent
and still echo through generations.

You were what they feared:
A girl who didn't flinch.
A girl who didn't fake it.
A girl who wore vulnerability like a
diamond…
flawless, and cutting.

Foxy,
you are the prayer I whisper
when I need to walk into a room
with both rage and radiance in my
step.

You are the reminder
that truth doesn't always come in
volume…
sometimes it comes in venom and
velvet.

And for every Black girl
who was told to hush her hunger,
you made it holy to crave.

You are still echoing.
Still shining in the hush.
Still Foxy.

Still fire.

For Xscape
The Harmony That Healed the Hard Places

You weren't just a girl group…
you were a God-send
to the girls who cried in silence
and the boys who needed someone
to translate ache into harmony.

You showed up
like a balm wrapped in bass.
Tiny voices with colossal truths,
melodies stitched from the middle of
the chest,
where pain sleeps
and love never quite forgets.

Xscape,
you taught us that harmonizing
wasn't just musical…
it was spiritual.
A form of survival.
A way to say,
"I miss you,"
"I forgive you,"
"I deserve better,"
without choking on the words.

You weren't about polish.
You were about presence.
About telling the truth in a key
that cracked ceilings
and made 'round the way girls
feel like royalty.

Your voices braided grief and
gumption.
Your stories weren't fiction…
they were what happened
in bedrooms, in backseats, in broken
homes.
And we listened
because we recognized ourselves.

You were the soundtrack to real
love.

Not the pretty kind.
The kind that bruises, begs, and still
believes.

And when you sang,
even our mothers paused.
Even our fathers looked up.
Because you held something ancient
in your cadence.
A holy ache.
A healing.

You didn't just Xscape the
industry…
you escaped definition.
You were too big for the box.
Too true for the mold.

And for that,
you remain a hymn in our hearts…
not just of what we went through,
but what we survived.

For Total
The Pulse Between the Bassline

You didn't just step in…
you slid through the smoke,
with lips lined in defiance
and voices dipped in velvet and
voltage.

You were the rhythm before the beat
dropped.
The breath before the kiss.
The unspoken truth behind every
girl's calm stare
that says, "I know my worth…
but I also know how to walk away in
silence."

Kima, Keisha, Pam…
You weren't backup.
You were the blueprint.
Black girl frequency
with no apologies attached.

Your harmonies didn't beg…
they declared.
Declared that softness had steel in it.
That attitude was armor.
That love could come with rules
and rhythm.

You were the fly girls on the block
who could sing you down,
stare you up and down,
and leave you haunted for decades.

You made hip-hop feel like silk.
You made R&B wear Timberlands.
You made us believe that power
could have a pout and still press
play.

And when your voices met…
it wasn't just harmony.
It was hypnosis.
A vibration that wrapped around us
like a slow grind we weren't ready to
stop.

You taught the girls
how to match mystery with melody.
How to make a whisper feel like a
prophecy.
And how to glow in the dark
without losing your bite.

You didn't chase spotlight…
you became the atmosphere.
And in that,
you carved a place
in the canon
for girls like us
who wanted to be seen and left
alone.
Wanted love,
but on our terms.

Total,
you were the mood.
The memo.
The mouthpiece for women
who knew that being unforgettable
was always better than being
understood.

For Ashanti
The Bloom That Sang in Silence

You were the hush before
heartbreak,
the echo after the voicemail played
twice,
the girl who made waiting feel sacred
and taught us that soft didn't mean
small.

Ashanti,
you were the melody beneath the
noise,
the hook that held the song together,
the backbone they borrowed
but rarely gave name to.
But we saw you.
We always saw you.

You walked in like the quiet girl
no one expected to lead…
until your pen bled platinum
and your voice whispered healing
into every speaker on the block.

You gave us love songs
that didn't demand
but invited.
Lyrics that sounded like diary pages,
folded with care
but lined with lessons.

You were never the storm.
You were the aftermath…
where everything was clearer,
where the air smelled like truth,
and even the silence had harmony.

You gave the girls permission
to be feminine in full.
To rock bamboo earrings
and still write poetry on napkins.
To mourn without drama,
to glow without competition,
to love again…even when it hurt.

You didn't shout your brilliance.

You bloomed it.
Softly. Steadily.
Like a rose that knew
the world wasn't ready
for a flower with that kind of power.

And now?
We know what you did.
We know you were never just a
feature…
you were the foundation.
The slow wine.
The sweet revenge.
The one who sang the truth
we weren't brave enough to say out
loud.

Ashanti,
you were the girl we loved to sing
with
and the woman we learned to heal
through.

You didn't just make music…
you made memory.
You made magic.
And we remember.

For Gabrielle Union
The Radiance That Refused to Dim

You didn't just survive.

You outshone
what was meant
to silence you.

Because survival alone
does not explain
this kind of light.

There were moments
meant to reduce you.

To make you smaller.
Quieter.
Easier to overlook.

But something in you
refused adjustment.

Not loud.

But certain.

You understood early
that dimming
is a negotiation.

And you chose
not to participate.

So you carried yourself
like light does.

Unapologetic.
Uncontained.

Even when the room
was not ready.

Even when the weight
would have been easier
to fold under.

You did not collapse.

You concentrated.

Turned pressure
into clarity.

Turned doubt
into direction.

And what they thought
would break you

became the reason
you glow differently now.

Because radiance like this
is not surface.

It is earned.

It is what happens
when someone refuses
to let darkness
decide their depth.

You are not just visible.

You are undeniable.

For Le'Andria Johnson
The Oil That Wouldn't Stay Quiet

You didn't come here to be polite.
You came to rupture.
To remind us that God speaks in gravel,
in grit,
in voices that sound like they've bled before.

Le'Andria,
you are not just anointed…
you are evidence.

Proof that the pulpit
was never meant to be pristine.
That deliverance ain't always pretty…
sometimes it sounds like a scream
and feels like a scar opening wide enough
for heaven to crawl through.

You sang what most are afraid to pray.
You drank. You broke. You bled truth.
And still, the oil found you…
again and again and again.

You taught us that sanctification isn't silence…
it's honesty.
That some of the holiest people
know how to cuss and cry in the same breath.

You baptized us in raw.
You reminded us that being chosen
has nothing to do with being polished.

You are the altar.
You are the ark.

And when you open your mouth,
it's not just song…it's soul.

For Keke Wyatt
The Woman Who Sings Like It's Survival

Keke,
your voice does not warm up.
It arrives.
Full.
Unapologetic.
Uncontained.
You don't sing notes…
you wrestle them into submission.
You bend them.
You stretch them.
You make them testify.
There is something almost spiritual
about the way you use your gift.
Like you understand
that your throat is altar.
They've called you dramatic.
Too much.
Too emotional.
But what is soul
if not emotion unfiltered?
You have never minimized your volume
to make others comfortable.
You cry when you need to.
Laugh when you want to.
Love loudly.
Sing louder.
And through every public storm,
every headline,
every misunderstanding….
your voice remained intact.
That's strength.
Keke,
you are not polished for approval.
You are raw by design.
And when you sing,
it feels like somebody
finally telling the whole truth.

For LisaRaye
The Diamond in White

They never saw
the discipline behind your dazzle.

The prayers
pressed into your posture.

The battles
carried quiet
like wings.

White was never just color on you.

It was intention.

A declaration
of clarity
in a world
that profits
from distortion.

You wore it
like armor made soft.

Like elegance
with memory.

You walked through Hollywood
with the South Side
still in your body.

Grace
with edge.

Velvet
over steel.

They called you a video vixen.

They needed a smaller word.

You were blueprint.

You were the moment
we realized
we could be seen
as luxury
without explanation.

Because you did not ask
to be redefined.

You stood.

And let perception
adjust.

In your silence
there was command.

In your gaze
there was knowing.

That we were always royal.

Even
when we had to polish
our own crowns.

For Da Brat
When I Saw Me in a Fade and a Fit

Before I had words for who I was,
I had her.

Baggy jeans.
A snatched fade.
A look that said,
"I'll outshine you in my own lane…
and won't explain a damn thing."

Da Brat didn't walk into rooms…
she clapped back at the concept of categories.

She wasn't soft.
She wasn't hard.
She was the space in between
where power lives comfortably
in cornrows and combat boots.

She gave me blueprint without blueprint,
a reason to feel fine in my skin
even when the world asked me to choose a side.

When I saw her,
I saw me…
in a universe that hadn't named me yet,
but already held a mirror.

She made me want to sag my pants and stand tall.
To flirt with confidence,
to flash a grin that said,
"Don't box me. Just admire."

She didn't just bend gender…
she rejected gravity.
Floated above expectation,
and still hit every beat like a war drum.

Da Brat didn't try to fit.
She made the fit conform.

And now, when I shine?
Know she's stitched somewhere in the lining of that light.

For Blaque
The Soundtrack of a Soft Revolution

Before the timelines.
Before the streaming charts.
Before nostalgia became currency…
there were three girls
who looked like us
and sounded like tomorrow.
Blaque wasn't just a group.
You were possibility.
You were harmonies braided tight,
confidence in crop tops,
femininity that didn't ask for permission.
You made teenage Black girls feel glossy.
Feel chosen.
Feel like the camera could love them too.
There was sweetness in your sound,
but don't mistake it…
there was discipline underneath it.
There was rehearsal.
There was grind.
There was ambition in those melodies.
You moved between film and music
like it was natural…
because it was.
You weren't loud.
You weren't scandalous.
You weren't built on chaos.
You were clean vocals,
tight choreography,
and a kind of sisterhood
that felt aspirational.
And even after the industry shifted,
even after time tried to blur the edges…
we remember.
We remember the hooks.
We remember the faces.
We remember the feeling.
Blaque,
you were the soundtrack
to a generation
learning how to glow up softly.
And that glow?
Still lingers.

For Destiny Child
The Discipline of Destiny

Before the crowns
there was harmony
Before the spotlight
there was faith
Before the world learned your names
you were already becoming
You were formation
before language could hold it
Voices layered like stained glass
each note catching light
without losing itself
Precision in heels
Softness sharpened into skill
Grace that knew how to stand
even when watched
Every era carried its own breath
Latoya
Latavia
Kelly
Michelle
Not departure
but turning
Like seasons that do not apologize
for becoming what they must
Because destiny does not fracture
It refines
Each woman distinct
yet moving like one current
Not sameness
but alignment
A sacred knowing
of when to rise
and when to release
You made survival sound like
rhythm
Independence feel like inheritance
Sisterhood move like strategy
not sentiment
Matching outfits
but never matching spirits
Because unity
was never about uniformity

It was about intention
You were not just a group
You were a blueprint
stitched in discipline
and carried in harmony
And even now
when the first note rises
It does not echo
It summons
And we do not remember
We return

For Robin Givens
The Woman Who Survived the Narrative

Robin,
they tried to write you into a cautionary tale.
Tried to shrink your name into scandal.
Tried to reduce you to headlines.
But you outlived the story.
There is something powerful
about a woman who survives public misunderstanding
and does not collapse.
You were young.
You were brilliant.
You were ambitious.
And ambition in a Black woman
has always unsettled fragile rooms.
They painted you sharp
because you refused to be silent.
They called you calculating
because you refused to be controlled.
But here's the truth …
you were educated.
You were strategic.
You were ahead.
You walked through fire
with cameras rolling.
And still,
you rebuilt.
Robin,
your resilience is quiet now.
Measured.
Seasoned.
You are proof
that surviving the narrative
is a form of victory.
And history has begun correcting itself.

For FeFe Dobson
The Girl Who Refused to Fit the Mold

FeFe,
you were Black and alternative
before the culture knew what to do with that.
You stepped into pop-rock spaces
that weren't built for your reflection
and you didn't ask permission.
You were eyeliner and edge.
Guitar and vulnerability.
Melancholy and defiance.
There was loneliness in your sound.
A kind of beautiful isolation.
You were the misfit
who gave other misfits a mirror.
You proved that Black girls
don't have to choose between softness and distortion.
Between beauty and rebellion.
You were ahead of the algorithm.
Ahead of the rebrand.
And now?
The world is finally catching up
to the lane you carved.
FeFe,
you were never niche.
You were necessary.

For Amiyah Scott
The Woman Who Claimed Her Visibility

Amiya,

you did not become visible.

You refused to disappear.

Before language caught up,
before rooms learned your name,
you stood
fully formed
in a world that preferred you edited.

There is a particular courage
in being seen
when being seen
can cost you everything.

You carried that cost
like silk

not because it was light
but because it was yours.

You did not ask for entry.

You altered the doorway.

Made space
where there was only tolerance.

Made presence
where there was only permission.

You did not ask to be seen.

You made invisibility obsolete.

Elegance, but never apology.

Femininity, but never performance.

Confidence that did not explain itself
to anyone committed to
misunderstanding it.

You existed
and the world had to adjust its
vocabulary.

Because of you,
visibility stopped meaning exposure

and started meaning power.

Amiya,

you are not a moment.

You are a shift.

And every woman
who now walks in truth
without shrinking to survive it

is walking
through a door
you held open
with your name.

For Jada Pinkett Smith
Perfecting What refused to Break

Let the truth be told
She was forged
before she was ever famous
Baltimore in her bones
grit in her mouth
a spirit that learned early
how to stand
without being held
She did not come from softness
She created it
Piece by piece
breath by breath
through rooms that tested
how much of herself
she was willing to keep
They saw Hollywood
She felt the cost
The smiling
The shaping
The constant negotiation
between who she was
and who the world could handle
She did not always get it right
But she never stopped
getting back up
This is not a story of perfection
This is a story of return
Returning to herself
after expectation
after heartbreak
after becoming
too many things
for too many people
She is not just resilient
She is aware
Aware enough
to name her fractures
without letting them define her
Aware enough
to sit with herself
when silence
was the only honest answer

She built a life
many dream of
But she also carried
what many hide
And still chose
to evolve in public
Not for approval
but because truth
was heavier than performance
She is not finished
She is refining
Learning
that healing is not a destination
but a discipline
That peace is not given
it is practiced
That love
must include herself
or it is incomplete
Let it be written
She did not break
where life expected her to
She became
Again
and again
and again
Blessed is the woman
who does not run from her
reflection
Who meets herself
fully
And still chooses
to stay
Because becoming
is not about getting it perfect
It is about refusing
to abandon yourself
while you figure it out

For Rachel True
The Girl Who Made Magic Look Like Ours

Rachel,

you were witchcraft before it was
aesthetic.

Before crystals were trending,
before alt-Black girl became brand,
you stood in the circle
calm, grounded, powerful.

In The Craft,
you weren't accessory.
You were anchor.

A Black girl in gothic space,
not asking permission to belong.

And that alone shifted something.

Because the world didn't always
imagine us
in dark lipstick,
in rebellion,
in mysticism that wasn't church-
bound.

But you did.

You carried cool without cruelty.
Strength without spectacle.
Mystery without apology.

And when the industry failed to give
you
the elevation you deserved….
you did not disappear.

You studied.
You evolved.
You deepened.

Tarot.
Spiritual literacy.
Self-knowledge.

You turned the narrative inward
and built power from within.

Rachel,
you were ahead of the conversation.

You made space
for Black girls who were different,
who were quiet,
who were observant,
who were powerful in ways
that didn't require volume.

You are not cult classic.

You are cultural imprint.

And for many of us,
you were the first time
magic
looked like us.

For Tink
The Winter Diary Queen from Chicago

Tink,

you write like snow falling on
concrete.

Cold.
Honest.
Unapologetic.

There's something Midwest in your
pen.
Direct.
Unfiltered.
No theatrics…. just truth.

You didn't just sing about love.
You documented imbalance.
Documented pride.
Documented the moment a woman
realizes
she deserves better.

Winter Diary wasn't just a series.

It was scripture for girls
learning how to detach without
hardening.

Chicago runs through your cadence.
Grit in the vowels.
Sorrow in the harmony.
Strength tucked between bars.

You never chased radio safety.
You chased honesty.

And honesty doesn't always trend.

But it lasts.

You write like someone who
understands
that heartbreak is curriculum.

That growth is rarely glamorous.

That softness can survive betrayal.

Tink,
you gave voice to the in-between
stage…
not fully healed,
not fully broken.

Just becoming.

And that becoming?
It resonated.

You are diary and discipline.
Confession and control.

The Winter Diary Queen from
Chicago
is not a nickname.

It's a title earned
by every woman
who found herself
between your lines.

For Angie Stone
An Angel Disguised as a Sacred Mirror

You did not sing to us
you restored us
Before the world named us threat
before silence became our armor
you spoke into the fracture
and called us whole
Brutha was never just a song
It was a hand on the shoulder
of every Black man
who forgot his own name
in a country that kept renaming him
A sermon
without a pulpit
A prayer
without permission
A mirror
that did not flinch
You said Brutha
like it meant lineage
like it meant legacy
like it meant
I see you beyond what they've done to you
And he felt it
In barbershops
in quiet drives
in the still moments
where he could finally exhale
without defense
You gave language
to dignity that had been
spoken over
written out
and still refused to die
Angie
you did not just hold a note
you held a people
And now that you have transitioned
your voice does not leave
It settles
in every man
who stands a little taller
because somewhere in his spirit
you are still saying
Brutha

For Mýa
The Woman Who Chose Stillness Over Noise

Mýa,

you were never meant to be loud.

You were meant to be precise.

There is something ancient in your
restraint.
Something deliberate in the way you
move through the world…
like a woman who understands that
preservation
is power.

They saw the dancer.
The choreography.
The beauty.
The early 2000s glow.

But they missed the monk.

They missed the discipline behind
your softness.
The spiritual isolation behind your
independence.
The choice …..yes, choice…
to step away from machinery
that would have devoured your
autonomy.

You did not burn yourself for
relevance.

You protected your light.

That is divine intelligence.

You walk like someone who knows
her body is temple.
You sing like someone who
understands breath is sacred.
You operate like someone who
values alignment over applause.

There is no desperation in your
legacy.

No frantic energy.
No need to compete.

You do not chase frequency.

You hold your own.

And that's why you've never
collapsed.

You chose ownership when it wasn't
trendy.
Chose self-containment when chaos
would have sold more records.
Chose silence when noise would
have paid faster.

Mýa,
that is spiritual sovereignty.

You are not just an artist.

You are a woman who refused to let
the industry fracture her identity.

And on a soul level,
that is rare.

You move like someone who
remembers who she is.

And because you remembered…
you endured.

Not as headline.
Not as controversy.
But as vibration.

And the ones who can feel it
know.

You were never background to an
era.

You were alignment within it.

For Mellow Buckzz
Eastside Crown

Mellowbuckzz,

you don't rap like you're asking.
You rap like you're collecting.

Eastside in your lungs,
block heat in your cadence,
steel in your syllables.

Your voice doesn't tiptoe.
It stomps.
It knows concrete.
It knows sirens.
It knows how to stretch a dollar
and shrink a doubt.

But beneath the bass
is the softness you guard.

You are grit with a pulse.

You learned early
that tenderness in certain zip codes
has to wear armor.
So you forged yours in rhythm.
Turned survival into cadence.
Turned pressure into posture.

You are claiming space
for the girls who grew up fast,
who learned to read rooms
before they read books,
who loved hard
and learned to hide it.

There is force in you.

Not loud for attention.
Loud for protection.

And even steel has a seam.

The power is not in the flex,
the chain,
the stance,
the glare.

It is in the fact
that you are still here.

Still rising.
Still sharpening your pen
instead of letting the city dull you.

You are not Eastside Queen
because you survived.

You are Queen
because you transmuted it.

Pain into presence.
Hunger into hunger for more.
Silence into sound.

Your throne is not velvet.
It is brick.
Cracked pavement.
Studio lights at 2 a.m.
The long road nobody posts.

And you sit on it
with your back straight.

That is royalty.

And whether they crown you now
or later,
the force is already in your hands.

Eastside does not whisper.

It reigns.

For Macy Gray
The Sound of Being Different

You made being different
sound like freedom.

That voice
raspy, textured, unbothered
never tried to fit into anyone's mold.
And that was the point.

You didn't polish your edges.
You made them your signature.
You didn't soften your tone
to make anyone comfortable.
You let it crack.
Let it stretch.
Let it tell the truth.

There is rebellion in your sound.
Playfulness in your presence.
An almost childlike honesty
that refuses to perform perfection.

You showed us
that artistry doesn't have to behave.
That beauty doesn't have to be
symmetrical.
That cool doesn't need permission.

You walked into rooms
with that hair, that sound, that stance
and dared the world
to adjust.

And it did.

Because authenticity
is louder than imitation.
And courage
is contagious.

You never chased mainstream
approval.
You let the mainstream chase you.
You never diluted your weirdness.
You amplified it.

And in doing so,
you gave so many of us permission
to breathe as we are.

To sound like ourselves.
To dress like ourselves.
To be strange.
To be soulful.
To be uncontained.

Macy,
you are proof
that originality ages beautifully.
That difference is not a flaw
it's a fingerprint.

You didn't just sing songs.
You created space
for misfits to feel magnificent.

And that?
That's legacy.

For Tabitha Brown
Let The Record Show

Let the record show
She did not rise by force
She rose by faith
Not loud
Not rushed
But steady in seasons
that told her to quit
She stood anyway
And God honored
what she refused to abandon
She is not just a woman who made it
She is a woman who waited
without losing herself
Who chose peace
when pressure demanded
performance
Who kept her softness
when the world rewarded hardness
Her kindness is not weakness
It is obedience
A discipline
A decision
A refusal
to let pain rewrite her nature
She walked through rooms
not built for her
And instead of asking for space
she became it
Doors opened
because her presence
was already an answer
She did not just build a brand
She built proof
That grace can scale
That faith can sustain
That purpose
does not require you
to betray yourself to reach it
She mastered something rare
How to win
without losing her spirit
How to rise
without hardening her heart
So let it be written
She was never too late
She was always on time
for the life that required her to trust
first
Blessed is the woman
who kept her spirit intact
And still built something
the world could not ignore

For Sarah Jakes Roberts
Not Survival, But Calling

She was never meant
to be a quiet miracle

Grace wrapped around history
Oil resting in places
people tried to call ruined

They thought her story was a warning
God called it a weapon

She does not speak from perfection
She speaks from excavation

From nights that asked questions
faith had to answer without proof

She does not walk in as someone who made it out
She walks in as evidence

That God does not consult your past
before assigning your future

She is not just resilient
She is responsible

For the women
still sitting in versions of themselves
she refused to stay in

She carries what many tried to hide
and names it without shame

Not to be seen
but so others can finally see themselves

She does not carry perfection
She carries permission

To rise unfinished
To be called anyway

She was not saved to be silent

She was sent
to remind you

what God touches
does not stay broken

The Legacy Lineage

"Honoring the Elders and Archetypes….Those Who Walked So We Could Rise

Before the spotlight, there was fire.
Before the fame, there was faith.
Before the freedom we now taste,
there were women who planted it….bare-handed, back-bent, barefoot if necessary.

This chapter is dedicated to the matriarchs of movement and elegance…those whose
very existence was political, poetic, and prophetic."

For Whitney Houston
The Sound God Trusted Most

You were the breath before the
miracle.

Whitney,
you didn't sing songs…
you breathed heaven into them.
Every note, a cathedral.
Every run, a revelation.
Every silence between verses,
a visitation from the divine.

You were proof
that God still speaks in melody.

You didn't just have range…
you had reach.
Your voice found the aching in us,
the aching we didn't have language
for,
and gave it wings made of wind and
wonder.

You made the impossible sound
effortless…
and that effortlessness?
It wasn't ease.
It was calling.
It was weight.
It was the echo of every Black girl
who had ever been told to dim…
suddenly glowing with no apology.

And when you sang "I Will Always
Love You,"
it wasn't just a ballad.
It was a Black woman claiming her
exit
with dignity so loud,
even silence stood up and clapped.

Whitney,
they called you "The Voice"
because there was no other name
for what happens when the Holy
Ghost decides

to put on a sequined gown
and sing through a woman.

Even in your softness,
you roared.
Even in your ache,
you ascended.

You reminded us that purity and
power
can live in the same chord,
that gospel never leaves us…
it just puts on pop's red lipstick
and dances barefoot through every
genre.

We did not deserve you.
But you gave anyway.

And now,
every time a Black girl
belts from the bottom of her
becoming,
every time a queer boy mimics your
high note
in the privacy of his deliverance,
every time a body shivers
from the sound of just one line…

we know:

Whitney was here.

And still is.

For Maya Angelou
The First Tongue That Knew Me

You walked through flame
barefoot,
unapologetically whole,
carrying scars like scripture,
not hidden,
not softened,
but spoken.

And you taught me
that survival is not quiet.
It is not just enduring
what tried to undo you.

It is alchemy,
turning grief into gospel,
turning silence into sound,
turning a body that was told to
disappear
into something that refuses to be
unseen.

That a caged bird does not sing
because it is free,
but because something in her
refuses to forget the sky,
even when the world
keeps trying to shrink it.

You gave rhythm to my rage,
not to tame it,
but to make it speak.

You gave softness
a spine,
taught it how to stand
without apology.

And you showed me
how to carry dignity
even when my name
shakes in unfamiliar mouths,
even when it is mispronounced,
misplaced,
or spoken like it does not belong to
me.

I did not just read your work,
I recognized it.

Like a memory
my body had been holding
long before I knew how to reach for
it.

Because it was already written
in the underside of my ribs,
in the quiet places
where survival lives without
applause.

And now, as I rise,
not perfectly,
not without trembling,
but still rising,

you rise again with me.

Not behind me.
Not above me.

But within me,
in every word I refuse to swallow,
in every truth I choose to tell
even when my voice
is still learning how to stay.

For Debbie Allen
The Pulse of Purpose

You made discipline look like dancing,
and precision feel like praise.
You didn't just walk into rooms…
you choreographed history.

Debbie,
you are the heartbeat behind the scenes,
the rhythm in the breath of the next Black girl
who dares to take up space
with sweat, grace, and grit.

You gave us not just steps…
but standard.
Not just stage…
but structure.

You are the reason so many of us
don't just show up…
we arrive,
head held high, knowing we belong
because you built the floor we dance on.

You are the movement in my voice,
the count behind my manifestation.
You are the pulse in my excellence,
and the proof that greatness
can be grounded and still fly.

For Debbi Morgan
The Woman Who Held Us Through It'

Debbi,

you don't just act.

You carry memory.

There is something ancestral in your
face.
Something that feels like it has lived
before the script ever arrived.

For decades,
you have embodied Black
womanhood
in all its contradiction…
devotion and exhaustion,
forgiveness and fury,
strength and collapse.

And you never caricatured it.

You respected it.

You made mothers feel sacred.
Made broken women feel layered.
Made survival feel honorable.

In a culture that often reduces Black
women
to either martyr or villain,
you gave us humanity.

And humanity is revolutionary.

You showed us that love can endure
betrayal.
That grief can coexist with grace.
That dignity can survive humiliation.

There are women who saw
themselves in you
and didn't feel ashamed anymore.

That is not small.

You are generational glue.
A face that anchored households.
A voice that steadied narratives.

Debbi,

your impact is not loud…
it is foundational.

You made Black women feel
witnessed.

And being witnessed
is a form of healing.

For Diana Ross
The Woman Who Became Possibility

Diana,

you were not just famous.

You were expansion.

Before you,
there were limits placed on how far a
Black woman
could ascend in public.

After you,
the ceiling cracked.

You didn't just sing…
you curated vision.
Hair, silhouette, posture, gaze…
every detail intentional.

You made glamour political
without announcing it.

Because to see a Black woman
command global adoration
with elegance and control
in that era
was rebellion.

They wanted you grateful.

You were sovereign.

They wanted you interchangeable.

You became irreplaccable.

There is something mythic about
you…
not because you were untouchable,
but because you understood visibility
as strategy.

You carried the Supremes.
You carried solo stardom.
You carried scrutiny.

And through all of it,
you never let the world see you
shrink.

You taught us that ambition
is not arrogance.
That style is armor.
That reinvention is survival.

But beyond the spectacle,
there is something even deeper.

You gave Black girls
a vision of glamour
that did not require proximity to
whiteness
to be validated.

You were center.
You were standard.
You were dream.

Diana,

your impact is cellular.

It lives in the confidence
of every Black woman
who walks into a room
knowing she belongs there.

Not because she was invited.

But because she exists.

That is soul recognition.

For Diahann Carroll
Silk with a Spine

You did not arrive.

You were already the standard
waiting for the room to catch up.

Diahann,

you wore elegance
like it had lineage.

Not costume
inheritance.

Your voice did not rise.

It clarified.

Cut clean through expectation
and left refinement where resistance
once stood.

You understood something early

that access is not given
it is assumed
until the world is forced to agree.

You did not soften to be accepted.

You refined the terms.

On screens that were not built to
hold you
you did not adjust your brilliance

you expanded the frame.

Silk, yes.

But tensile.

Threaded with discipline,
with study,
with a knowing that beauty
without intellect
is decoration

and you were never décor.

You were design.

You taught us
that grace is not passive

it is controlled force.

Measured.

Intentional.

Unshakeable.

Heels were not ornament.

They were punctuation.

Every step
a sentence the industry could not
ignore.

You did not ask to belong.

You made belonging look
insufficient.

And now

every woman
who enters a room
without shrinking her excellence

is speaking
in a language
you made fluent.

For Ruby Dee
The Voice Between the Lines

Ruby,

your words did not begin with you.

They arrived
already carrying memory.

Every line you touched
held the fingerprints of ancestors

inked in struggle
and still legible in grace.

You did not perform.

You translated.

Turned breath into witness,
silence into testimony,
and presence into something
history could not ignore.

Your voice knew weight.

Not volume
weight.

The kind that settles in a room
and rearranges what truth sounds
like.

You gave us resistance
that did not shout
but endured.

Dignity that did not bend
but moved
like water carving stone.

You were never just an actress.

You were passage.

A crossing
between what was suffered
and what refused to stay silent.

You made us look longer.

Feel without defense.

Understand that love
in a world that denies it
is its own form of revolution.

Ruby,

you did not speak lines.

You made language accountable.

And even now,
your voice does not echo

it continues.

In every artist
who refuses to soften truth
to be accepted.

In every story
that insists on being told whole.

You are not remembered.

You are referenced.

The ink in our conviction.

The breath in our defiance.

The pause
where truth gathers itself
before becoming change.

For Kim Wayans
The Precision of Funny

Kim,

you were never just "the sister."

You were surgical.

Your comedy had intelligence in it.
Timing that felt studied.
Character work that felt lived.

On a stage built for chaos,
you brought control.

You stretched faces.
Bent voices.
Shifted bodies into caricature…

and still kept dignity intact.

There is something masterful
about making people laugh
without making yourself small.

You didn't need vulgarity to be bold.
You didn't need spectacle to be sharp.

You made absurdity artful.

And beyond the sketches,
there was depth.
Drama.
Range.

Kim,
thank you for showing us
that Black women in comedy
can be layered.
Disciplined.
Unapologetically skilled.

You were never background energy.

You were foundation

For Patti LaBelle
The Voice That Could Command Heaven

Patti,

you don't sing.

You ascend.

There is thunder in your vibrato.
Church in your chest.
A wail that feels like it traveled
through generations before reaching us.

You don't perform emotion…
you unleash it.

When you hold a note,
it feels like surrender and dominance
at the same time.

You are drama in silk.
Grandeur without arrogance.
A diva who earned the title
before the industry learned the word.

You survived eras.
Labels.
Trends.
Reinventions.

And still…
that voice remained sovereign.

You taught us that soul requires courage.
That range requires discipline.
That longevity requires backbone.

Patti,
you are not just a singer.

You are standard.

A blueprint for how to command space
without asking permission.

And when your voice rises…
rooms still shift.

Because greatness
recognizes no expiration date.

For Cicely Tyson
The Face of Forever

You wore history on your face
and made it look like purpose.

Cicely…
your roles weren't characters,
they were callings.
You didn't act,
you embodied.

You showed us that dignity wasn't performative…
it was ancestral.
That we don't beg for roles,
we birth them from our bones.

You spoke slowly,
but your impact struck like thunder.
Every time you appeared,
we felt our mothers,
our grandmothers,
our future daughters
stand *taller.*

You are the lineage in my walk,
the prayer behind my poise,
the armor in my silence.

You didn't just walk so we could rise…
you *rose* so *we* could soar.

For Sheryl Lee Ralph
The Woman Who Refused to Dim

You were the sound my spirit made
before I ever had a mouth,
before I understood
what it meant to be overlooked
and still show up shining.

Before I could name the feeling
of being passed over,
you wrapped it in a voice
that refused to be quiet,
and sang it back to me
like joy was not something
anyone could take.

As if you had always known
that being unseen
would try to teach me
to disappear.

You walked into rooms
that did not expect you to last,
did not expect you to rise,
did not expect you
to become undeniable.

And still
you stood there
unmoved,
unshrinking,
unwilling to fold yourself
into something easier to accept.

You did not dim.
Even when the lights
were never meant for you.

And you taught me
that waiting is not the same
as becoming smaller.

That being overlooked
does not mean you are not worthy
of being seen.

That sometimes the world
does not clap

because it does not yet understand
what it is witnessing.

You gave rhythm to resilience
without turning it into struggle.

You gave joy
a backbone,
showed me how to laugh
without forgetting
everything it took to get there.

And you showed me
how to carry presence
even when the room
has not yet decided
to make space for you.

I did not just watch you.
I recognized you.

Like a future
that refused to give up on me
even when doubt
tried to rewrite the story.

Because something in me
had already decided
I would not disappear
just because I was not immediately
chosen.

And now, as I rise,
not because they called my name,
but because I answered it myself,

you rise with me.

In every space
that tried to overlook me,
in every moment
I chose not to shrink,

in every version of myself
that refused
to be dimmed.

For Phyllis Hyman
The Voice That Outlived the Room

Phyllis,
you were too much for one plane.
Too velvet.
Too thunder.
Too honest for this world
that asks women to sing and suffer quietly.

You didn't.

You opened your mouth
and the entire room shattered…
not from volume,
but from truth.
A truth that came wrapped in satin
and storm.

You sang with the weight of ancestors
clinging to your diaphragm.
And when you cried in song,
the floorboards remembered their purpose.

But pain, too, is a song.
And it was yours to carry
until the silence felt safer than the sound.

Phyllis,
you were not broken.
You were beyond this world's reach.

And we,
those who arrived too late to touch your hem,
still feel your echo when jazz leans into blues.
When glamor aches.
When beauty sings with a bruise under its eye.

You are not gone.
You are gospel to the misread.
A psalm for the overfelt.

And I want you to know,
we heard you.
Even when the world didn't.

For Ava DuVernay
The Director of Destiny

You didn't just hold the camera…
you rewrote the script of the cosmos.
Where they erased us,
you resurrected us in full color,
in full knowing,
in full glory.

You made quiet girls feel loud.
You made loud girls feel sacred.
You made sacred girls feel seen
without needing to be softened.

When you yell "Action,"
the ancestors lean in.
The lens becomes a portal.
Time folds to your will.
Black women become myth again…
not because they are imagined,
but because they are finally remembered.

Ava,
you taught us that direction is not just where we're going,
it's how we are framed
on the way there.

You didn't just give us a seat at the table…
you built the whole damn set.
And called "Lights!"
on all the ways we've been dimmed.

You turned our struggle into cinema,
our breath into score,
our magic into a movement.

For Loretta
The Incantation of Warmth

You entered every room like gospel.
Not to be heard.
To be felt.
your voice is a lullaby that braided
the pain out of the world
and kissed joy into its scalp.

Loretta,

your name hums
like bedtime prayers,

like sweet potato pie
cooling on a windowsill
no one ever rushed.

You have been
every auntie,
every soft place,
every story
the world tried to forget
but you carried anyway
until it could breathe again.

There is magic
in your laugh.

Not loud.

But loosening.

The kind that shakes sorrow
out of the body
without asking permission.

There is power
in your presence.

A mother tongue
we never had to learn
because it already lived in us.

Your art is ancestral.

Your cadence
a quilt.

Each word
a thread
stitched carefully
into who we are becoming.

And whether they told you or not,

you have been
a kind of shelter.

A divine softness
for generations
of Black children
who didn't know
what they were missing
until they felt you

and recognized it
as safety.

For Phylicia Rashad
The Woman Who Stood Like a Cathedral

Before we had language for grace,
you were already standing in it.

Not performing dignity
embodying it.

Clair Huxtable was not simply a
character.
She was architecture.

The way you entered a room
was not entrance
it was alignment.

Back straight.
Voice measured.
Eyes steady with the knowing
of a woman who answers to no
smallness.

You did not shout to command respect.
You breathed it.

And in every courtroom scene,
every dining room correction,
every soft, intelligent laugh

you redefined Black womanhood
without spectacle.

You made elegance look inherited.

But beyond the scripts,
beyond the applause,
beyond the awards

there is something deeper.

A philosophy.

"The universe bears no ill to me,
so I bear no ill to it."

That is not passivity.

That is sovereignty.

That is a woman who understands
that bitterness is not a crown worth
wearing.

You moved through industry storms
without venom.

Through criticism
without collapse.

Through misunderstanding
without shrinking.

Because you understood something
sacred:

Peace is power.
Composure is rebellion.
Grace is defiance.

You did not mirror the chaos around
you.

You stood like a cathedral.

Unmoved by weather.
Unbent by opinion.
Anchored in self-trust.

Little Black girls watched you
and saw intellect paired with tenderness.
Authority paired with warmth.
Strength paired with serenity.

You were not a stereotype.

You were a standard.

And standards do not age.

They endure.

Relics are not old objects.
They are sacred artifacts
that remind us who we are
when we forget.

And you, Phylicia Rashad,
are a living relic.

A woman who chose grace
in a world addicted to reaction.

A woman who bears no ill
because she understands
that the universe reflects what we carry.

And so you carry light.

And so we follow.

For Lucinda Moore
Safe Was Not Just a Word

Lucinda,

Safe in His Arms was not just a song
to me.

It was shelter.

There were seasons when life felt
loud,
unstable,
uncertain…
and that record didn't just play.

It held me.

You didn't rush that song.
You didn't overpower it.
You let it breathe.

Every phrase felt intentional.
Every pause felt prayerful.
Every run felt like reassurance.

You sang it like someone
who understood the weight
of the word "safe."

Because safety is not softness.
It is relief.
It is exhale.
It is finally putting your guard down
when the world has required you
to stay armored.

There were days I didn't have
language
for my exhaustion.
But when you sang,
it translated.

You didn't dramatize the pain.
You didn't perform theatrics.

You ministered steadiness.

That song felt like being covered.

Like being reminded
that collapse was not the end…
that there was somewhere
to fall.

Lucinda,

you took your time.

And that's what made it powerful.

You didn't treat the melody like a
platform.
You treated it like responsibility.

You sang like someone
who knew somebody listening
needed it to be real.

I was somebody.

There are moments in life
where faith feels fragile.

And your voice
kept mine intact.

Not because it was loud.
But because it was anchored.

You didn't just sing about
protection.

You sounded like it.

And that…
that got me through.

For Deborah Wilson
The Woman Who Disguised Genius as Comedy

Deborah,

you shapeshifted.

Not lightly.
Not lazily.
But fully.

Voices.
Posture.
Presence.

You didn't parody…
you embodied.

In rooms that rarely give Black women
permission to be outrageous and brilliant at once,
you claimed both.

There is courage in transformation.
In taking up physical space.
In refusing to be typecast
as the "safe"Funny woman.

You went big.
You went bold.
You went technical.

And it mattered.

Because mimicry is skill.
Impression is study.
Satire is intelligence.

Deborah,
thank you for being fearless with your range.

You proved that Black women
can be absurd, sharp, exaggerated, precise…
without losing respect.

That's mastery.

And mastery
doesn't fade.

For Octavia Spencer
The Power of Truth

Before the statues
and the golden applause,

there was a woman
walking quietly through rooms
the world had not yet learned
how to see.

Octavia Spencer
a voice steady as oak,
a presence grounded
like roots beneath deep soil.

You did not arrive
as a whisper.

You arrived
as truth.

And truth,
when spoken with courage,
has a way of shaking
even the oldest walls.

When you brought Minny to life,
you gave the world
more than laughter
and more than rage.

You gave us a woman
whose dignity could not be erased
by injustice.

A woman who understood
that strength
sometimes wears an apron,
sometimes carries pain,
sometimes delivers justice
with a pie and a quiet smile.

Because your art
has never been about spectacle.

It has been about honesty.

About revealing the humanity
inside stories
that history tried to hide.

Octavia,

you showed us that greatness
does not always arrive

in towering figures
or booming voices.

Sometimes greatness
looks like persistence.

Like a woman
who keeps showing up,
keeps believing in her craft,
keeps trusting
that her moment will come.

And when it did
the world stood.

Not just for the award,
but for the journey.

For the reminder
that talent and perseverance
are a force no gatekeeper
can hold back forever.

Now the doors
that once seemed locked
open wider.

And young artists
watching from living rooms
learn something powerful:

That brilliance
does not require permission.

That stories matter.

That authenticity
will always outlive doubt.

Octavia Spencer,

your legacy is not just the roles
that made audiences feel.

It is the truth you carried
into every frame

that a woman who stands
fully in her purpose
can change the entire story.

And the story
is better
because you told it.

For Anna Maria Horsford
Matriarch of the Living Room

You were never just a character.

You were the couch cushion that
held a whole generation's weight.
The kitchen table where discipline
met love.
The voice that could correct you
without breaking you.

When you played Dee,
you didn't act.
You archived us.

You preserved the sacred rhythm
of Black womanhood in domestic
spaces
the sighs,
the side-eyes,
the way love could sound sharp
but feel like protection.

You were the balance in a house full
of fire.
The quiet thunder.

And when you became Mrs. Jones in
Friday,
you reminded the world
that Black mothers carry both humor
and holiness.

You made us laugh
but you also made us remember
that there is always a woman
holding the structure together.

You were never background.

You were blueprint.

Every "boy, please."
Every knowing glance.
Every layered tone
became cultural scripture.

You didn't just play mothers
you modeled matriarchy.

And that matters.

Because little girls saw authority
wrapped in grace.
And little boys saw correction
wrapped in love.

You stood in rooms where Black
women were often caricatured
and you chose depth instead.

You chose dignity.

You chose dimension.

And in doing so,
you carved space for generations
of actresses to exist as full human
beings.

Not tropes.
Not punchlines.
Not shadows.

Relics are not dusty.

Relics are sacred objects that survive
time.

And you, Anna Maria Horsford,
are not nostalgia.

You are living history.

You are the matriarch
who taught us that strength can wear
curlers
and still command a kingdom.

You are the lesson.
The laughter.
The lineage.

And we thank you.

For Shonda Rhimes
The Woman Who Rewrote the Script

Shonda,

you didn't just create shows.

You restructured power.

Before you,
Black women on primetime were
limited to archetypes.
Supporting. Secondary. Simplified.

After you?
They were surgeons.
Fixers.
Professors.
Complex.
Desirable.
Dangerous.

You didn't ask the industry to widen
its lens.
You forced it to.

There is something surgical
about your storytelling.

You cut into morality.
You dissected ambition.
You let women be flawed without
punishment.

And that changed everything.

You made Black women lead
without apology.
Without softening their edges
to make viewers comfortable.

You trusted our intelligence.
You trusted our contradictions.
You trusted that we could hold
power
without being likable.

That trust mattered.

You built worlds
where competence was sexy.
Where vulnerability was layered.

Where ambition wasn't villainized.

Shonda,
you didn't just write television.

You expanded imagination.

And generations of women
are walking into rooms differently
because they saw your characters
survive them.

That is architecture.

That is influence.

That is legacy

For Mama Tina
The Woman Who Raised Empires

You are the kind of woman
who turns survival into silk.

Not loud about it.
Not asking to be seen.
Just steady.
Rooted.
Regal in the way
only mothers of empires understand.

You did not announce grace.
You embodied it.

You modeled softness
without ever shrinking.
Taught strength
without ever hardening.

There is something about you
that feels like porch wisdom
and Paris couture
in the same breath.

You are legacy
that walks in lip gloss and prayer.

You did not just raise greatness.
You protected it.
Shielded it.
Watered it
when the world was not watching.

And while they celebrate the fruit,
I see the soil.

I see the hands that kept tending
when the harvest was not
guaranteed.
The patience it took
to believe in what had not bloomed
yet.

Mama Tina,
you are not just support.

You are structure.

The quiet architect behind
excellence.

The blueprint of elegant strength.
The proof that nurturing
is not weakness.

It is strategy.

Because empires do not rise
by accident.

They are prayed over.
Guarded.
Built in moments
no one records.

And you were there
for all of them.

So when the world stands
in awe of what grew,
I stand in reverence
of the woman
who never stopped planting.

May you feel the flowers
you placed in others
blooming back toward you.

Because what you built
was never temporary.

It was generational.

For A.J. Johnson
The Woman Who Stayed Radiant

Before the world learned your name
from the glow of the screen,
you were already walking
like a woman who understood light.

Not the kind from cameras
or flashing marquees

but the kind that lives
inside a person
who refuses to dim.

You stepped into stories
with laughter in your bones
and fire in your spine.

In rooms where women were told
to be small,
to be quiet,
to be background

you showed us
how to be center stage.

Sharane dancing through youth,
Yvette speaking truth with a fearless
tongue
you gave us characters
who felt like cousins,
like sisters,
like reflections in the mirror.

But your real magic
was never only acting.

It was the way
you carried yourself
long after the credits rolled.

A.J.,
you turned wellness into wisdom.

You reminded us
that beauty is not something
the world places on a woman

it is something
she cultivates.

Like breath.
Like strength.
Like peace.

You taught us that grace
is a discipline.

That joy
is a decision.

That aging
is not fading

it is expansion.

And somewhere,
in studios and living rooms
and quiet mornings
where women stretch toward their
best selves

your spirit is present.

Encouraging.
Radiant.
Unapologetically alive.

So thank you
for every role that made us laugh,
for every truth spoken without fear,
for every moment you reminded us

that a woman's power
is not in how long she shines

but in how boldly
she chooses to glow.

And you, A.J. Johnson,
have always been
a woman
made of sunlight.

For Holly Robinson Peete
Grace in Motion

Before the applause,
before the bright lights learned your
name,
there was already a quiet strength
walking beside you.

A grace
that did not ask permission
to be seen.

The world first met you
in uniforms and scripts
Officer Judy Hoffs
holding her ground with courage and
calm
a woman who could stand in the
storm
and still make it look like sunlight.

But Holly,
your truest role
was never written on a page.

It was written
in love.

In the way you chose your family
again and again
with a devotion
stronger than any spotlight.

When the world misunderstood
what it meant to raise a child
who sees the world differently,

you didn't hide.

You stood up.

You turned a mother's love
into a movement,
turning confusion into
understanding,
turning silence into awareness.

And suddenly,
thousands of families
who once felt invisible
found themselves
finally seen.

That is the kind of legacy
that cannot be measured in awards.

That is the kind of courage
history remembers.

Because beauty fades
from cameras and time,

but compassion
true compassion

echoes forever.

So thank you, Holly Robinson Peete,
for showing us
that strength can be gentle,
that advocacy can be fierce,
and that a woman can carry
both fame and purpose
without losing her soul.

You are not just an actress
or a voice on a screen.

You are proof
that grace, when guided by love,
can change the world.

And somewhere tonight
a mother breathes easier,
a child feels understood,
and a family stands stronger

because you chose
to shine your light
beyond the stage.

And that light
will never fade.

For Shawnna
First Lady of the Flow

Shawnna,

before the city started shouting
about who runs Chicago,
you were already in the booth
writing your name in ink that
wouldn't wash off.

You didn't ask to be "the female
version."
You stepped in as the standard.

Your pen was sharp
not gimmick sharp,
not cute sharp
surgical.

You could flirt on a hook
and body a verse in the same breath.

That duality?
That was power.

You carried Chicago in your delivery
that fast-talking, no-nonsense
cadence,
that Midwest confidence
that doesn't beg coastal approval.

You were rapping next to giants
and never shrinking.

That matters.

Because the industry loves to make
women accessories
to male brilliance.

But you were never an accessory.

You were architecture.

You showed girls from the city
that intelligence could be sexy,
that humor could be lethal,
that wordplay didn't have to sacrifice
femininity.

There was hustle in your tone.
Ambition in your posture.
Strategy behind the swagger.

You weren't just making songs.

You were claiming territory.

And even when the spotlight shifted,
even when the narrative moved on,
your imprint didn't.

Chicago remembers.

The girls who study cadence
remember.

The ones who want bars
and beauty
and brains in the same package
remember.

Shawnna,

you didn't just rap.

You set a precedent.

And that kind of influence
doesn't expire.

It echoes.

For Quinta Brunson
The Woman Who Made Genius Feel Familiar

Quinta,

you didn't knock on the door.

You built the building.

There is something radical
about the way you make brilliance
approachable.
The way you let humor carry truth
without diluting it.

You understood early
that laughter opens minds
faster than lectures ever could.

And so you taught us…
through awkward pauses,
through side-eyes,
through the sacred chaos of
underfunded classrooms
and overworked hearts.

You didn't make comedy small.
You made it precise.

You honored everyday Black
excellence.
The teachers.
The caretakers.
The ones who show up anyway.

You didn't chase prestige…
you defined it.

And when success came,
you didn't abandon the room you
came from.

You brought us with you.

There is humility in your confidence.
Intelligence in your silliness.
Strategy in your joy.

Quinta,
you remind us that representation
doesn't have to be heavy
to be meaningful.

That genius can be warm.
That leadership can be playful.
That Black women can build empires
without hardening themselves to do
it.

You didn't just make us laugh.

You made us feel seen.

And that….
that's cultural care

For Pam Grier
The Woman Who Made Freedom Look Like Fire

Pam,
you didn't just step on screen…
you kicked the door open.

Before "empowerment" became marketing,
you were living it.
Leather, ammo, eyeliner….
and a stare that said
I will not be handled.

They wanted Black women grateful.
Quiet.
Safe.

You showed them dangerous…
not reckless,
but sovereign.

You made desire political.
You made strength glamorous.
You made survival look like style.

And the industry tried to profit off your nerve
without honoring the cost of it.

But legacy doesn't ask permission from disrespect.
Legacy outlives it.

Pam,
you are not a symbol.
You are a source.

Every time a Black woman leads with audacity,
your fingerprints are somewhere in the frame

For Toni Braxton
The Voice That Broke Beautifully

Toni,

you never had to run.

Your voice walked in slowly.
Low.
Smoky.
Certain.

There is something sacred
about a woman
who doesn't oversing.

You don't chase notes.
You let them unfold.

That contralto?
It doesn't beg for attention.
It commands atmosphere.

You made heartbreak elegant.

Not hysterical.
Not theatrical.
Just… honest.

When you sang about love,
it sounded like surrender.
When you sang about loss,
it felt like dignity.

There is power in restraint.
And you mastered it.

You carried vulnerability
like silk over bone.
Soft, but structured.

And even when life pressed hard…
financial storms,
public scrutiny,
health battles…

your tone never fractured.

It deepened.

Toni,
you taught us
that softness can still be strength.
That sensuality can still be sorrow.
That quiet women
can still dominate a room.

You were never loud.

You were layered.

And when your voice enters…
the world doesn't just listen.

It leans in.

For Taraji
The Alchemist of Every Room

Taraji,
you didn't just walk in…
you arrived.
You burned a path through the cold
and made the world feel again.

You are not just a woman,
you are what happens
when God throws audacity into a
womb
and says,
"Now go…show them joy with
thunder in it."

You make vulnerability holy.
You laugh with your whole body,
like your ancestors are clapping
behind your teeth.
You cry like gospel…
like healing is possible
even after the silence.

You taught the world
that strength can wear lashes and
heartbreak
at the same time.
That a woman can be soft and steel,
can crack open and still carry
everyone she loves across the finish
line.

You have been the blueprint for
surviving
with soul intact.
The voice that doesn't tremble
even when the world does.
The friend we see in every character.
The cousin. The sister. The mother.
The fighter. The phoenix.
The truth.

Taraji, you are more than an
actress…
you are a sermon in motion.
You remind us that Black women
don't need saving…
they are the saviors.

That love can be fierce
and still forgiving.
That broken doesn't mean buried…
it means becoming.

So here's to the girl who didn't let
the system
swallow her.
To the woman who made Cookie a
household name
but never let her outshine Taraji.
To the way you carry grief like grace,
and still make room for joy.

May this poem kiss the cheek
of the little girl who once cried in
silence.
May she now know…
she didn't survive in vain.

You were made
for this.
You were made
to shake stars out of their hiding.
You were made
to show the world
what love looks like
when it's been through hell
and still walks in
wearing gold.

For Viola Davis
The Little Girl Who Carried the Fire

Before the Emmys,
before the fences,
before the world remembered to
bow
when you walked in…

there was a little girl
in South Carolina heat,
carrying hunger in her stomach
and galaxies in her eyes.

Viola…
you were born a storm wrapped in a
whisper.
Born with ribs that knew ache
but a spirit that refused to fold.

This poem is not for the world-
renowned actress.
This is for the girl in you
who stood in silence
while life threw too much, too soon.
This is for the child
who tried to find God in cracked
ceilings
and strength in locked bathrooms,
who learned too early
how to survive
and forgot for a while
how to simply be.

But we see her now.
I see her.

I see the way she still lives in your
tears
when you win,
in your laugh that breaks the air wide
open,
in the way you hold your power like
it's sacred..
because you know it came
at a price.

Viola,
you gave a voice to every woman
who thought pain was their only
language.
You gave brown girls the right
to be complex,
to cry and curse and shatter
and still be worthy of the frame.

But this..
this right here…
is for the barefoot, beautiful girl
who just needed someone to say:

You were always enough.
You didn't need to prove it.
You didn't need to earn love.
You were the light before they saw
it.
You were the masterpiece before
they framed it.

I write this to your marrow,
to the brave, breathing child
still curled inside your ribcage.
May she stand tall now.
May she dance.
May she run free through every line
you speak
and every set you stand on.

Viola…
you are the legacy
and the little girl.
You are the thunder
and the tenderness.
You are seen.
You are loved.
You are home.

For Tichina Arnold
The Laugh Was a Weapon

Your laugh was never just joy.

It was armor
dressed up in something easier to
swallow,
something people could accept
without asking questions
they were never ready to hear.

You laughed
before they could notice the shift in your
voice,
before silence had the chance
to expose what you were holding.

You laughed
so no one would ask
if you were tired,
if you were breaking,
if there was something underneath
you did not have the language
or the safety
to explain.

It was sharp.

Precise.

Timed perfectly
to redirect attention,
to keep the room light
even when you were carrying
something heavy enough
to pull you under.

And they mistook it
for ease.

For comfort.

For a life untouched
by the things that teach you
how to survive quietly.

But I see it.

The way your laughter
arrived just a second too early,
the way it lingered
just long enough
to keep people from looking closer.

The way it filled the room
so completely
that no one noticed
what was missing from you.

Because laughter like that
is not careless.

It is learned.

Built
in moments where truth
felt too dangerous to say out loud.

Built
in rooms where softness
was not protected.

Built
in a world that taught you
how to perform ease
instead of being allowed
to fall apart honestly.

Your laugh was a weapon
because it had to be.

Because it kept you safe.

Because it gave you control
in spaces that were never designed
to hold you gently.

Because it let you exist
without being questioned
too deeply.

But I wonder
who you are
when you do not have to laugh first.

When you do not have to soften the
moment
before it softens you.

When silence
is not something to escape
but something that can finally
hold you.

For Tisha Campbell
The Voice That Carried Us Through Chaos

You gave us vocals
before we knew how to name tone,
before we understood
that a voice could carry more than
sound,
that it could hold truth
without asking for permission.

You gave us Gina
before we had the language
to call something complicated,
before we understood
what it meant to love someone
who did not always know how to
love themselves back.

You gave us realness
in an industry that survives
by teaching people how to pretend.

You could laugh and cry
in the same breath
and make both feel necessary.

Not dramatic.
Not excessive.

Just honest
in a way that made it impossible
to look away.

Because there is something sacred
about someone who does not hide
what most people are taught
to bury.

You were never trying to be perfect.
You were trying to stay whole
in spaces that reward performance
over truth.

And we felt that.

We loved you for that.

Because we saw ourselves

in the cracks you did not cover,
in the moments where strength
looked like simply not disappearing.

Your voice held ache
that did not always get
acknowledged.

Your roles held soul
that people sometimes consumed
without recognizing the cost.

Your face held truth
even when the script
tried to smooth it out.

And still
you kept showing up.

Not untouched.
Not unscathed.

But present.

Beautiful in a way
that does not erase what you have
been through,
but carries it
without apology.

Bruised, yes.
But blooming anyway.

And that is what stayed with us.

Not just the laughter.
Not just the voice.

But the fact that you did not let
what tried to break you
take your sound with it.

And you are still here.
Still rising.
Still carrying every note
that refused to be silenced.

For Anita Baker
The Woman Who taught love and Wrapped it in Velvet

Anita,

your voice does not rush.

It knows.

It arrives
like something already understood
before it is spoken.

You do not chase crescendo.

You allow feeling
to gather
until it becomes undeniable.

There is discipline in that.

A refusal
to confuse volume
with truth.

You made romance feel
intentional.

Not frantic.
Not pleading.

But chosen.

As if love
were not something to fall into

but something
to stand inside of
with both feet.

When you sing,

time does not move forward.

It deepens.

And "Angel"
is not a song.

It is a remembering.

My mother
in the living room,

eyes soft
with something I did not yet have
language for,

holding a love
that did not need to announce itself
to be eternal.

That kind of love
does not arrive loudly.

It settles.

In the way she looked at me.
In the way she did not have to say
"I will stay"

for me to know
she already had.

You gave sound
to that silence.

You made space
for the kind of devotion
that does not perform

but protects.

That does not beg to be seen
but remains.

You understood

that intimacy
is not spectacle.

It is presence.

And presence,
when held long enough,

becomes legacy.

Anita,

you are not excess.

You are precision.

A reminder
that love does not have to reach
to be felt.

It only has to be true.

And truth,

when carried gently enough,

lasts longer
than anything
that ever needed to shout.

For Chaka Khan
The Woman Who Is the Fire

Chaka,

you are not a voice.

You are combustion.

From the first note,
there is no negotiation.

Power.
Range.
Soul that refuses containment.

You don't enter songs..
you overtake them.

There is something ancestral
about your sound.
Church and funk.
Freedom and ferocity.

You made sensuality bold.
Made power feminine.
Made range unapologetic.

You didn't smooth your edges
to be palatable.

You roared.

And in that roar
was liberation.

You sang like a woman
who understood that her gift
wasn't decoration…
it was weapon.

Chaka,
you are rhythm and rebellion.
You are vulnerability without
weakness.
You are control without restraint.

And when you open your mouth,
it doesn't feel like performance.

It feels like eruption.

You didn't just influence R&B.

You ignited it.

For Tasha Cobbs Leonard
The Sound That Shattered Silence

You opened your mouth…
and generations were set free.
Not just the saints in pews,
but the secret-keepers,
the broken daughters,
the Black boys who'd forgotten how to cry
without shame.
You sang like a woman who had survived her own flood,
and came back carrying lifeboats.
Tasha…
you don't just hit notes.
You part seas.
You don't just worship.
You *war*.
We didn't always know what deliverance looked like
until we heard it…in your holler,
in your stillness,
in the cracking of your own voice
as you called on a God who never left you.
You reminded us:
Glory doesn't always wear gold.
Sometimes, it wears sweat, and stretch marks,
and a shout so loud it scares the pain out of the room.
You are the storm *and* the healing.
You are oil *and* fire.
You are the altar
and the reminder
that we've always been holy.
When we couldn't find the words,
you wept for us.
When we didn't know how to pray,
you screamed our name in tongues.
So this love letter is wrapped in a choir robe
stitched with gratitude.
You've carried us through breakups, funerals,
births, breakthroughs…
and still, your voice stands tall
like a lighthouse in the midnight hour.
We see you.
We honor you.
We rise with you.
Because when *you* open heaven…
we all get in.

For Yolanda Adams
You Sound Like Sunday

Your voice could part Red Seas,
not just in scripture,
but in us.

In the quiet places
where we were drowning
and needed something
to open.

You did not just sing gospel.
You stretched it
until it reached people
who did not even know
they were looking for God.

You made it sound like jazz,
like breath,
like something alive.

You made it sound like freedom,
like a body finally loosening
what it had been holding all week.

You made it sound like survival,
like something we could carry
from Sunday
into everything that tried to break us
after.

You gave us God
in a way we could feel.

Not distant.
Not unreachable.

But close.
Wrapped in velvet,
steady in soprano,
rising in notes
that felt like they knew exactly
where we hurt.

You were the altar
in a world too loud to pray,

in a life that did not always leave
room
for stillness.

And somehow
you made space anyway.

Inside a song.
Inside a breath.
Inside a moment
where everything finally
stopped fighting us.

When you opened your mouth,
it was not just sound.

It was release.

It was the kind of silence
that comes after crying
when you finally feel
held.

And we still play your voice
when the world gets heavy,
not out of habit,
but out of knowing.

Because something in us
remembers
what it feels like
to be lifted
without having to explain
why we were low.

Because you do not just sound like
Sunday.

You sound like mercy.
Like rest.
Like a door opening
in a room we thought
we were stuck in.

For Tamela Mann
You Sang Us Back to Ourselves

Your voice is a homecoming.
A cry we all recognize.
A wail that leads us back
to the God we forgot we needed.

You didn't just sing "Take Me to the
King"…
you took us.

Past pride.
Past performance.
Past the mask we wear in public
and the ache we hide in private.

You carried us
into surrender.

You are what a storm sounds like
when it's cleansing.
You are what grief becomes
when it's baptized.

When you open your mouth,
it is not entertainment…
it is excavation.

You pull the sorrow up from the
ribs.
You drag the shame out of the
throat.
You make grown people cry
without embarrassment.

There's no performance in your
praise.
Only power.
Only testimony.
Only a woman who has lived
what she sings.

You don't decorate the melody.
You wrestle it.
You pray through it.
You bleed through it.

And somehow
your strength never hardens.

It softens us.

You sang with your whole life….
marriage,
motherhood,
loss,
faith that had to survive doubt.

And we felt every breath of it.

You are not just a gospel singer.

You are a bridge.

Between despair and deliverance.
Between exhaustion and renewal.
Between the version of ourselves
that broke
and the version that stands back up.

Tamela,

when you sing,
we remember who we are.

And sometimes….
that is the miracle.

For Michelle Obama
The Garden That Grew Beyond Concrete

You were never just a title.
You were translation.
Of discipline into grace.
Of pressure into poise.
Of history into something that could
stand tall and breathe.

They said South Side
like it was a ceiling.
You heard South Side
and built language out of it
brick by brick
until even the cracks had music.

You turned concrete into cultivation.
Not by escaping it
but by understanding it.
By knowing what it takes
for something soft to survive
in a place that was never meant to
hold it.

There is a precision to the way you
move.
Nothing accidental.
Every word measured
like you knew the weight of being
heard
before the world decided to listen.

You did not rise loudly.
You rose correctly.
With intention that could not be
rushed
and a steadiness
that made even doubt feel
temporary.

You taught us
that legacy is not something you step
into
It is something you shape
with quiet hands
and an unshakeable sense of self
until it becomes undeniable.

You are not a moment.
You are method.
Not just presence
but proof
that excellence can be both rooted
and expansive at the same time.

And in a world that often confuses
visibility with value
you reminded us
that growth does not ask permission.

It insists.

And because of you
we understand something deeper
now

We were never too much
for the spaces we entered

The spaces were simply
not built for our becoming

For Alfre Woodard
When God Made Grace, He Whispered Her Name

You walked into the frame,
not to perform…
but to prophesy.
With a voice like sweet thunder
and eyes that knew stories
we hadn't even remembered yet,
you gave us dignity
without needing a monologue.
You gave us *presence.*
A Black woman who could shift a room
without raising her voice,
yet when she did…
heaven stood up
and hell sat down.
They call it acting.
But we know better.
You were conjuring.
You were channeling.
You were holding space for the ancestors
while teaching the next generation how to breathe.
You are the kind of woman
they study in silence
because words fall short.
You are Sunday dinner and courtroom justice,
you are jazz riffs and protest chants,
you are what happens
when a spirit doesn't bend
in a world that tries to fold us.
No award
can ever contain
what you've given us.
You were never trending…
you were *timeless.*
Not built for red carpets,
but altars.
So here.
Let me say it plain.
You are love.
You are adored.
You are valued.
And your work…
your very *being.…*
will never, ever be erased.

For Toni Morrison
She Wrote Us Back to Ourselves

She did not write stories.
She **remembered us out loud.**
Before we had the courage
to say our names without apology,
she was already
building sentences
that refused to bow.
Ink in her hands
did not behave like ink
it moved like memory
that survived something.
She wrote
like silence owed her something
back.
And every page
felt like a door
we didn't know
we were allowed to open.
She did not ask
to be understood.
She demanded
to be **felt.**
Blackness in her work
was not struggle alone
it was texture.
it was breath.
it was language
before language
was softened
for other people's comfort.
She gave weight
to the things
we were taught to carry lightly.
Grief.
Motherhood.
Desire.
Memory.
She said
these are not burdens.
these are archives.
And suddenly,
we were not just living.

We were being **documented.**
There is a difference
between being seen
and being written correctly.
She did both.
Her words did not chase beauty
they **redefined it.**
In scars.
In silence.
In survival that did not ask for
applause.
She taught us
that language could hold us
without shrinking us.
That a sentence
could be a home.
That we were not too much
we were **too precise for the world**
that tried to misread us.
And even now
her voice does not echo.
It **remains.**
In the way we speak truth
without softening it.
In the way we remember
without asking permission.
In the way we write ourselves
into spaces
that once refused to hold us.
She did not just leave us books
…she left us
a way
to never disappear again.

For Tasha Smith
Fire With Structure

You are fire
that learned how to behave
without ever losing heat.

Intensity
with direction.

Power
that does not spill over,
but lands exactly
where it is meant to.

Every role you touch
feels lived in.

Not imagined.
Not borrowed.

But earned
in places
people do not see.

Fought for
in ways
people do not ask about.

There is something about your presence
that does not need explanation.

It says
you have been through something
that tried to quiet you
and failed.

It says
you know exactly
what it costs
to stand up in yourself
without apology.

You carry strength
like someone
who had to build it
piece by piece.

Not given.
Not assumed.

Built
after being broken
in ways
that do not leave visible marks
but change everything.

You do not just act.

You take space.

You do not ask
to be felt.

You make it impossible
not to.

You do not perform emotion.

You bring it with you.

You let it sit in your body
long enough
for it to become real
to anyone watching.

And behind that boldness
is something quieter.

Discipline
that does not announce itself.

Craft
that does not beg to be seen.

Work ethic
that lives in the repetition
no one applauds.

Tasha,
you are not just reinvention.

You are what it looks like
to refuse
to stay in the version of yourself
that the world felt comfortable with.

You are resilience
that did not harden into bitterness.

You are softness
that did not disappear under pressure.

You are control
without losing feeling.

You are what it looks like
when survival
puts on lipstick
stands up straight
and decides
it will not break
again.

For Whoopi Goldberg
The Woman Who Became Institution

Before the EGOT,
before the panels,
before your voice became something
people expected to hear,

you stood alone.

Not polished.
Not packaged.

Just certain
in a world that does not reward
certainty in women
who refuse to be softened.

You did not fit.

And you did not try to.

You did not round your edges
to make yourself easier to hold.

You did not chase approval
from rooms that were never built
to understand you fully.

You built anyway.

You moved between comedy and
drama
like neither one could contain you,
like category itself
was too small a box
for what you carried.

Because what you had
was not performance.

It was perspective.

You spoke
when silence would have been easier.

You challenged
when agreement would have kept you
safe.

You made yourself visible
in ways that do not come without
consequence.

And still

you did not step back.

Because being you
was never about being liked.

It was about being true
in a way that does not bend
when the room shifts.

You are not a trend.

You are what remains
when trends fade.

You are what stays
when the noise moves on.

And that kind of presence
does not come without cost.

It comes from years
of being misunderstood,
misread,
and still choosing
not to explain yourself
into something smaller.

You carry decades
not lightly,
but honestly.

Like someone who knows
what it took
to get here.

And whether they agree with you or
not,
whether they understand you or not,

they must acknowledge you.

Not because you asked them to.

But because you never asked
for permission to exist
in the first place.

And that
is legacy.

For Shoniqua Shandai
The Woman Who Glows Loud

You are electricity
but not the kind that arrives without warning.

The kind that learned
how to light itself
after being left in the dark
too long.

Your joy is not accidental.

It is chosen
again and again
in a world that gives you
every reason
to dim it.

You enter rooms
like color that refuses
to be corrected.

Not softened.
Not filtered.

Just present
in a way that makes everything else
adjust.

You are rhythm
in human form.

Not just sound
but timing.

Knowing when to laugh
and when to hold it back
so it means something.

Knowing when to be light
and when to stand still
inside your own weight.

Volume with heart.

Confidence
that does not need to cut
to prove itself.

But do not mistake that
for ease.

Because there is something underneath
that people do not always see.

The discipline
it takes
to stay open.

The decision
to remain joyful

without pretending
you have not been hurt.

There is something magnetic
about your authenticity
because it does not feel performative.

It feels earned.

Like something you had to return to
after it was challenged,
after it was questioned,
after it was almost taken from you.

You do not shrink
to be digestible.

But I know
that was not always easy.

I know there were moments
where it would have been simpler
to be quieter,
to be smaller,
to be less.

And you chose otherwise.

You celebrate loudly.
You love loudly.
You live loudly.

Not because you do not know pain
but because you refuse
to let it dictate
the volume of your life.

And in a world
that polices Black women's joy
like it is something dangerous,

you expand anyway.

Not recklessly.

Intentionally.

You are not too much.

You are what it looks like
when someone stops apologizing
for taking up space.

You are not just enough.

You are proof
that enough
was never the standard
you were meant to live by.

For Pour Minds
The Gold That Flows

Draya.
Lex.

Before people learned how to listen to
women
without trying to correct them,
you were already speaking.

Not to perform.
Not to impress.

But to pour.

They saw the name first.
Pour Minds.

And still missed it.

Because pouring is not emptiness.
It is overflow.

It is what happens
when you have too much truth
to keep inside your body.

You didn't build a podcast.

You built a space
where women could release
without being reduced.

No clean edits on emotion.
No permission slips for honesty.

Just voice.

Raw.
Unfiltered.
Alive.

And what you gave people
was not advice.

It was recognition.

The kind that sounds like:

"I thought it was just me."

That is currency.

Not quiet currency.
Not polished currency.

But something heavier.

Something that lingers

after the laughter fades.

Because what you pour
does not disappear.

It settles.

In language.
In memory.
In the way women begin
to speak to themselves
with less shame
and more truth.

Draya.
Lex.

You are not just talking.

You are translating experience
into something people can hold.

And that kind of work
does not expire.

Long after the episodes end,
long after the timestamps fade,

what you created
will still echo
in conversations you will never hear.

Because you did not just pour stories.

You poured permission.

And permission
is where transformation begins.

So let it be said clearly.

You are not Pour Minds
because you are empty.

You are Pour Minds
because you are full enough
to let it flow.

And what flows
like that

is never small.

It becomes legacy.

For K. Michelle
The Woman Who Stayed in the Story

K,

you did not wait
to become perfect
before you became visible.

You showed up
while it was still happening.

Not the polished version.
Not the healed ending.

The middle.

The breaking.
The choosing again.
The truth
while it was still uncomfortable.

You did not protect your image.

You told it as it was
and they called you too much
for refusing to be edited.

But what they were seeing
was a woman
who would not rewrite herself
for approval.

You did not perform strength.

You lived it
in real time.

You let history record you
as you were.

And that is legacy.

Not perfection.
Presence.

You are not remembered
because you were flawless.

You are remembered
because you stayed.

And that kind of truth
echoes.

In every woman learning
she does not have to be finished
to be real.

You are not a moment.

You are a record.

Of what it looks like
when a woman
lets her life unfold
without apology.

For Sheraseven
The Language of Worth

Before they turned your voice into a
phrase,
you spoke of value women had to
claim,
not something borrowed from
another's gaze,
but something rooted deeper than a
name.

They heard the surface, missed the
deeper thread,
reduced your language to a passing
tone,
yet you were shifting how a woman's
led,
teaching her she is not for all to own.

And they came for you, your choices
and belief,
your love, your home, the way you
chose to stand,
as if a woman firm must come with
grief
for daring not to shrink at their
command.

They questioned softness shaped
within your frame,
mistook restraint for something less
than fire,
not knowing stillness can outlast the
flame
and quiet standards can redraw desire.

You held a mirror many feared to face,
not polished glass, but one that spoke
back truth,
reflecting patterns time could not
erase,
the learned acceptance dressed as
second youth.

You spoke of worth, but also how to
build,
of mind, of means, of structure, not
just stance,
that value, once awakened, must be
filled

with discipline, with choice, with
circumstance.
Not every woman liked what you
revealed,
not every ear was ready for your tone,
for some, your words uncovered what
they sealed,
and forced a reckoning they called
your own.

And still you stood, composed within
your frame,
a quiet mystery they could not define,
where allure moved softly without
asking claim,
and power never begged to be seen as
shine.

You were not here to soften every
truth,
nor make it easier to be received,
you spoke to those prepared to face
their proof,
and left the rest to question what they
believed.

Not loud with praise, but steady, sure,
and true,
your impact lives in what they choose
to do,
a knowing glance, a standard
understood…

and just like that, sprinkle, sprinkle.

The Unwritten Names Still Bloom

If your name didn't echo through these pages,
don't think for one second your light went unseen.
This book was built on your shoulders too…
you, the rhythm in the silence between each poem,
the scent of shea and sandalwood floating between the lines.
You are not forgotten.
You are the reason the pen moved.
I may have missed the spelling,
but I never missed your presence.
Every wink you gave the camera,
every laugh you shared when the world was watching,
every boundary you broke…
your magic is stitched into this very fabric.
You, who mothered me from a distance,
healed me without even knowing,
danced me through heartbreaks
and called me back to myself
when I almost forgot my name.
No shade lives here,
only the glow of reverence.
This was never about a roll call…
this was an altar.
And every single one of you sits upon it.
Thank you.
I see you.
I love you.
I wrote this for you, too.

The Echo I Leave Behind

"A personal closing section of poems from me to you...
for the girls who glisten, the boys who bloom,
the babies who bend gender into gold,
the ancestors who never missed a beat,
and the divine feminine magic that made all this possible."

To Future Black Girls You Are the Proof

You are not waiting to be
crowned…
you are born crowned.
And if they don't see it,
that's their blindness… not your
absence.
You are not invisible…
you are undeniable in rooms
that have not yet learned your
language.
You are laughter with depth.
You are sweetness that slices.
You are softness sharpened by
knowing.
You are the quiet storm
they mistake for stillness.
The kind of power
that doesn't announce itself..
it rearranges everything when it
arrives.
Let the world call you too much.
It's because they've only tasted dust.
They don't know what to do
with something that is both gentle
and unbreakable.
They don't know how to hold
a girl who refuses to shrink.
You are honey, salt, and revolution
all wrapped in braids, silk, melanin,
and memory.
You are legacy walking forward.
You are ancestors answered prayers.
You are every dream that refused to
die
taking shape in real time.
Don't shrink, baby.
Expand.
Expand past their expectations.
Expand past their projections.

Expand past the version of you
they are comfortable with.
Grow roots and wings at the same
time.
Be grounded in who you are…
and limitless in who you become.
You don't need permission to take
up space…
you are the space.
You are the blueprint
they will study later.
The standard
they will pretend they always
understood.
And when the world tries to humble
you
for shining too brightly…
remember:
You were never meant to dim.
You were meant to illuminate.
You are not becoming.
You are revealing.
And every step you take in your
truth
makes it easier
for another Black girl
to believe in hers.
So walk like it's already yours.
Speak like it's already known.
Move like you've already arrived.
Because you have.
You are not the exception.
You are the evidence.
You are the proof.

To Black Queer Boys Glitter Is a Weapon Too

You, with your light that bends the
rules,
your walk that turns concrete into
rhythm,
your laugh that defies gravity…
you were never meant to be
understood
by systems built to contain you.
You are not a side character in
someone else's story.
You are the author.
You are the plot twist.
You are the spell.
You are the moment
they try to name
but can't quite hold.
You are art that refuses to sit still.
A body that remembers joy
even when the world forgets how to
offer it.
They may try to dim you,
to box you in lace or shame or silence.
To make you choose
between softness and survival.
But baby…
you don't fit in boxes.
You set them on fire.
You turn limitation into language.
You turn rejection into runway.
You turn glitter into armor
and still manage to shine through it.
That is power.
Because what they fear most
is not your difference…
it's your freedom.
The way you exist
without asking permission.
The way you love
like the world hasn't tried to punish
you for it.
That is revolutionary.
That is sacred.

That is legacy in motion.
You come from a lineage
of boys who danced anyway,
who loved anyway,
who lived anyway…
even when the world tried to make
them disappear.
So when you step outside,
know this:
You are not too much.
You are the measure.
You are not extra.
You are abundance.
You are not fragile.
You are force wrapped in finesse.
Keep dancing.
Even when the floor feels uneven.
Keep loving
like nobody ever taught you how…
because truthfully,
they didn't.
They only taught you how to survive.
But you?
You chose to live.
And that choice…
that defiance…
that joy…
is louder than anything
they ever tried to silence.
You are freedom with a face.
A future that refuses to hide.
And the world…
whether it admits it or not…
is better
because you dared to exist.
So wear your glitter.
Not just as decoration…
but as declaration.
Because yes…
glitter is a weapon too.
And in your hands,
it becomes light

Final Dedication Page

For the Black women who mothered the world and myself...
in spirit, in style, in survival.

For the voices we heard before we had our own.
For the hands that fed us language,
the glances that made us sharpen,
the laughter that carried me through the dark.

To the ones who made magic look mundane
and greatness look casual.

You were never background.
You were the whole story.
This is my offering back to you.

Author's Note

I didn't write these poems to impress.
I wrote them to remember.
To return.
To reclaim the pieces of myself that were molded by women whose names often get mentioned last
when really, they were the first breath of the culture.

This book is more than a love letter.
It's a resurrection.
It's the sound of a Black boy growing into his own divinity
by tracing the fingerprints of the women who shaped his soul.

Some of these women raised me through screens.
Some through songs.
Some through ancestral code that pulsed through my blood
before I ever knew to call it power.

To those reading this:
May these poems light your memory.
May they melt your armor.
May they lift the veil and remind you
who the architects of your greatness truly were.

This is not just my story.
It's our altar.